Fair Warning
Leo Connellan and His Poetry

Fair Warning

Leo Connellan and His Poetry

Edited by

Sheila A. Murphy & Marilyn Nelson

Fair Warning: Leo Connellan and His Poetry

Layout & Design by Joe Zanghi
Cover photo by Sturgis Haskins

Printed Matter Press
Z Bldg. 2F,
2-8-14 Kitueno, Taito-ku,
Tokyo, Japan 110-0014

290 Somers Road
Ellington, CT
U.S.A. 06029

E-mail: info@printedmatterpress.com
http://www.printedmatterpress.com

First edition

Printed in Japan

ISBN 978-1-93360625-5

For Russ

If ever two were one, then surely we...

Sheila Ann

Table of Contents

Preface

In a pew at Leo Connellan's funeral, a cold, wet day, the thought came to me that someone should put together a posthumous *Festschrift* in Leo's honor. My suggestion was greeted enthusiastically by everyone I approached with it at the reception afterward, where we celebrated Leo's life and work, and at the sad burial with muddy shoes and upturned collars. But everyone said I was the one who should do it. By the grace of God, Sheila Murphy suddenly appeared in my life a few weeks later, inquiring about a different matter. When I asked her to co-edit a volume of essays about Leo, neither of us had any idea that I was dragooning her into several months of demanding work, much of it undertaken while Sheila was recuperating from first an automobile accident, then a bad fall. I wondered often, during Sheila's year of convalescence and editing, whether meeting and agreeing to help me wasn't another face of Sheila's spate of bad luck. I'd like to express here my gratitude to her and her wonderfully supportive husband, Russ, and to make clear to all readers the fact that in our partnership I was the grasshopper, and Sheila the ant.

Like several of the authors collected here, I was the recipient, often to my annoyance, of occasional telephone calls from Leo, during which he would go on and on, as I rolled my eyes, about how he had struggled to write his poems, welcomed as a compeer by only a handful of poets he invariably named at some point during the course of every call. For, perhaps because he lived outside of it, Leo was incapable of being dishonest about his sense that the business-world of contemporary American poetry is dominated by well-connected prize-winning workshop teachers and their prize-winning MFA-holding former students. Leo saw the poetry workshop as being valuable for its companionship, and for the access it provides to teaching jobs and readings. He much preferred students who went their own way to those who obediently took notes and followed orders. Only those courageous enough to bear the solitude of independence might, Leo thought, someday be poets. Students who, like Leo, went their own way. I was always grateful for the fact that he considered me one of these.

Leo went his own way. He was a loner, an outsider, a man who wrote poems not because he chose to, but because poetry was the central practice of his life. He wrote first—literally, between 5:00 and 6:00 in the morning—then he lived. He did not have an epiphany during his junior year of college, which made him decide to apply to a good MFA program, and become a workshop teacher publishing in good little magazines edited by former classmates and friends. Leo came to poetry the hard way: without a college degree and through struggles with unromantic poverty and alcoholism, the motherless son of a demanding father in a hard-scrabble fishing town on the coast of Maine. His poems are beautiful, not pretty. They do not play word-games; they were not inspired by visits to art museums. If they are about travel, they describe hitch-hiking across America not because it was a fun thing to do, but because he couldn't afford a bus ticket. His poems are exhausting, their jarringly odd and lovely phrasings and their tough honesty—not to mention their length—compelling attention even as they render up verbal delights and wise truths.

Knowing Leo was a difficult privilege. Yet the cantankerous, funny, insecure, driven man we knew and loved was only the smaller part of a much larger picture. The larger picture is the man's work. The small part died Leo's death, of a stroke, on February 22, 2001. The larger part, his gift of poetry, lives and waits to be discovered, again and again. I hope this volume of essays will bring more readers to Leo's poems.

Marilyn Nelson
Poet Laureate of Connecticut
April 15, 2003

Introduction

Lary Bloom, writing in the *Hartford Courant's Northeast Magazine* after Leo Connellan's funeral, reflected on "an incomplete Leo [whose] writing is eloquent, and important, but it never earned him the place he deserved." Marilyn Nelson, also appreciating Leo's "outsider" status, saw the need for a collection of essays about Leo's work to celebrate the hard-won achievement of his poetry and to introduce his poetry to new readers.

The initial call for manuscripts requested "critical appraisals." Some contributors, though, wanted to discuss the intersection of Leo's poetry and his life, or the intersection of their lives with Leo's. I came to accept that with this project, as with Leo, unpredictability would be the default. Indeed, the original publisher withdrew, and I was unsuccessful in my attempts to find another. When Jesse Glass came forward in 2009, I was grateful, although many more months of volunteer labor ensued.

These 20 new pieces and 15 reprints include reviews, interviews, evaluations, and reminiscences. The authors are poets who knew Leo well or from afar, teachers and lawyers, professors and students, family members and friends. Often, appraisal blends with memory as in Sydney Lea's "Whereas Leo...."

In the first essay, "My Head Swims in Music," John and Mary Abbott draw on their extensive "Leo Connellan file" to share elements of Leo's literary persona. They recommend book-length critical and biographical accounts that would "assess Leo's important place in American literature of the post World War II period." By exploring the richness of the poems and the complexity of the life that produced them, this collection makes a preliminary contribution toward that assessment.

Sheila A. Murphy
January, 2010

Photo by Arthur Simoes

Leo Connellan and His Poetry

"My Head Swims In Music": Some Material Pertaining to a Life of Leo Connellan

Mary and John Abbott

In the mid-twentieth century, poetical exegesis underwent a revolution defined principally by John Crowe Ransom in The New Criticism (1941) and later by Cleanth Brooks in *The Well-Wrought Urn* (1947) and William Wimsatt and Monroe Beardsley in *The Verbal Icon* (1954). These New Critics called for a direct address to the poem as a formal entity and favored a close line-by-line reading instead of explaining the poem through external matter. Chief among the1atter, of course, was biography itself, which heretofore was almost automatically invoked as a preliminary to reading a poem. Thus, any reader of "Ode on a Grecian Urn" knew that Keats died young; of *The Cantos* that Pound had disgraced himself by broadcasting for the Italian fascists during World War II; or of *The Wasteland* that Eliot sought a redefinition of self in assuming British citizenship. While such details were interesting, the New Critics argued they ultimately had nothing essential to do with a poem's value or meaning. That could properly be referred to the poem's immediate contents.

While the profound influence of the New Critics has never entirely waned, few would argue that it dominates the critical landscape as it once did. In fact, with the rise of the New Historicism, material collateral and external to poems, plays, and novels, particularly biographical information, is seen as essential. Samuel Johnson's *The Vanity of Human Wishes* cannot be meaningfully read, for example, without a knowledge of Juvenal's tenth satire or the various references that repeatedly inflect the poem, particularly lines 159-60—"There mark what ills the scholar's life assail,/Toil envy, want, the patron, and the jail." Without a knowledge of Johnson's letter to Lord Chesterfield of February 7, 1755, and his general uneasy relationship with his supposed patron, they have no real depth of meaning. Few would argue today, then, that serious poetic exegesis can take place without collateral resources, particularly biographical matter.

This is certainly the case with Leo Connellan's poetical canon. The latter is defined by historic duration (he engaged early in writing poetry and sustained his remarkable production to the end of a relatively long life). Equally, it is defined by a remarkable variety ranging from delicate, short lyrics to his celebrated trilogy, *The Clear Blue Lobster-Water Country*. Many of his poems are defined by direct if somewhat disguised use of biographical elements that tangibly shape a corpus of powerful poetic utterances. While his poetry has received extensive exegesis in a variety of formats, no single work is yet dedicated to assessing his important place in American literature of the post World War II period. Similarly, while the general outline of his personal and poetic life is detailed in a variety of sources, no sustained biographical account exists. Both books would do much to solidify, even elevate, the position that Leo achieved during his lifetime; he clearly deserves such critical and biographical treatment.

What we would like to suggest here is that abundant materials for his life exist, particularly since we assume we were not alone in having kept a good deal of material about Leo during the period we knew him well—from the spring of 1985 to his death in 2001. While keeping files on literary figures is a common habit for English teachers (our most voluminous include such figures as Fanny Burney, Samuel Johnson, George Orwell and Norman Mailer), keeping one on a contemporary author is perhaps somewhat more unusual. From the outset, though, there was always something special about Leo. In his poetry as in his person, we found Leo to be an artistic force field. We had, in fact, some literary basis for comparison in sharing common space, even personal conversation, over the years with such figures as Robert Frost, Stephen Spender, and Tom Wolfe. It is likely, however, that anyone reflecting on Leo and his remarkable career would have no trouble remembering his or her first encounter with him.

In Mary's case it happened somewhat accidentally when she attended, with no previous know1edge of the man or his poetry, a reading by Leo at Eastern Connecticut State University in April 1985. She returned that evening with the comment that she had "bought a poetry book." Somewhat out of professional obligation I said I would take a look at it. It was about 10 o'clock when I began reading *The Clear Blue Lobster-Water Country* and some two hours later when I finished it. It was a text I couldn't put down (the last such was James Dickey's *Deliverance)* and was the first component in the "Connellan file" that began that evening, one that was enriched in the months and years to come by a variety of letters, copies of manuscripts, journal tearsheets and newspaper accounts, photographs and other miscellaneous material that Leo routinely shared with us. We consider as an essential part of this file, of course, the numerous personal contacts we both had with Leo for a number of years. These included many extended conversations in person and by phone as well as his numerous classroom visitations. In effect, we have been able to gather over the years a substantial body of the same material that so enriched the first modern biography, James Boswell's *Life of Samuel Johnson*. Chief among these, of course, was the letter. While future biographers will find the traditional letter in an age of brutal and perishable e-mail a disappearing biographical species, Leo's life is expansively defined by such correspondence, often the best of biographical evidence—the autograph letter signed or "A.L.S." This kind of evidence is particularly valuable in combining authenticity (its provenance is certain) with the immediacy and vitality of the commentary ("hearing" the writer's voice) that epistolary novelist Samuel Richardson characterized as "writing to the moment." Leo wrote in a variety of paper formats—long letters typed (but not word processed on a computer) as well as long hand-written letters (always printed in a clear, distinct hand) and these were combined with brief notes, often postcards from a recent or current brief vacation. He often included as well copies of letters he had written to or received from others. The principal subject addressed in each letter was, not surprisingly, his poetry. He never strayed far from this subject, though it manifested itself in a number of ways. Equally, one often sees his ruminations on poetic theory and the creative process—the kind of thinking that characterized a canon of interviews that would certainly be invoked by his biographer. Certain letters contain glimpses, at least, of his early years of struggle now made somewhat more bearable by the success that came to him later in life.

Writing from New York's Omni Park Center Hotel, which he was enjoying on August 23, 1985 in luxury denied to him when he first lived in the metropolis, he notes: "There is nothing like seeing a place when you don't belong to it. It isn't often enough that we get to walk on top of our graves.—I am exactly where I actually was as a boy in 1949. Broadway curves, still, to where, then, I worked as a soda fountain sandwich man and short order cook, for one of the Walgreens. The drug store is gone, but not the skeleton of the street." The letter is suggestive, moreover, that Leo was perpetually a poet and wanted to share a recent effort. "Here is an example, an exercise I forced myself to do this morning," he wrote. "I write *every* morning, or I'll lose it. Especially if I must talk about it." On November 28, 1986, again reflecting on the poetic process he wrote that "On Sunday, November 30, I join Mark Twain and Winston Churchill having a birthday, my 58th!! The best present I could ever have is to hope that I've 'caught,' 'captured' at least one more poem! I tell myself that out of crudeness comes greatness, since the polished doesn't show the sweat it took; 'could be wrong!!'"

While optimistic utterances such as the above are seen with some frequency, it would distort the general tenor of Leo's correspondence to us to suggest that such optimism generally prevailed. On the contrary, Leo's letters often focus on what one might call the official poetic world in which he had to function for nearly half a century. Letters in our file, some of great length and real candor, will prove to be especially valuable to any biographer who wishes to provide a complete picture of Leo's place in what he saw as a highly politicized, often unfair community of essentially academic or "protected" poets writing from safe havens of tenured college and university appointments. While he acknowledges here those who tangibly came to his aid—including such figures as Robert Penn Warren. Richard Eberhart, and William Packard—he is scathing in noting those who from his perspective actively sought to block the recognition and awards that he felt he properly could claim.

While professional students of literary biography have long known that Boswell's *Life of Johnson* only appears to offer conversations as virtual on-the-scene transcripts (Boswell reconstructed as much as he transcribed Johnsonian utterances), his technique of making oral material an essential part of any biography has never waned, especially in an age of tape recordings. A far less tangible, yet essential part of our "Leo Connellan File" has to be referred to the fact that we spent dozens of hours in Leo's presence or talking with him for protracted periods on the phone. From this contact, as Boswell's with Johnson, we formed lasting impressions that ratified the first strong impressions Leo always generated. Attendantly, we had the advantage of seeing and hearing Leo in two different venues—for me it was in fairly frequent lunches for over ten years and frequent conversations by phone; for Mary it was her English classes at Windham High, to which Leo presented himself as a regular visitor/lecturer.

First impressions seem to remain the most distinct, however they are later refined. I still remember meeting Leo in April of 1985. After reading his trilogy I very much wanted to meet its author and joined Leo at Friendly's Restaurant in Willimantic in a lunch arranged by Mary. While some might automatically connect Leo's forceful handshake and direct eye contact as something out of his salesman's handbook, it was more essentially associated with the basic nature of the man himself. Intimations of friendship and respect, no less than desire itself, seem to manifest themselves in each of us no matter how much we call on reason to amend feelings we might not deserve or in any case should better avoid. In my own case, I felt an instant affection—I don't think the term is too strong—for Leo that increased rather than lessened over the years. For some reason then and persistently over the years, I was reminded in talking with and listening to Leo of Nick Carraway's words about Jay Gatsby in noting that "if personality is an unbroken series of successful gestures, then were was something gorgeous about him, some heightened sensitivity to the promises of life, as if he were related to one of those intricate machines that register earthquakes ten thousand miles away." Fitzgerald's poetic prose here has ever seemed apt to me in defining a poet capable of hearing voices near and far, and in so much brilliant verse giving them a local habitation and a home. The passage describing Gatsby continues in words once again appropriate, at least to the Leo I came to know over the years. "This responsiveness," Fitzgerald writes, "had nothing to do with that flabby impressionability which is dignified under the name of the 'creative temperament'—it was an extraordinary gift for hope, a romantic readiness such as I have never found in any other person and which is not likely I shall ever find again." A comparison yoking Leo Connellan to America's great novelistic poet and, arguably, modern fiction's greatest romantic could well seem excessive, though the latter should be a judgment reserved for those who knew him as we did. His poetic quest was such that he deserves to be included, at least, in that tribe of Romantics at whose head Jay Gatsby inevitably seems to take his place.

Usually one who by profession was heard to lecture, I listened far more to Leo than talked. While he was certainly in error in investing far too much in formal academic credentials or formal academic placement, I don't think I was ever in error in seeing at the outset a poet of extraordinary genius. On more than one occasion I reminded myself and shared the thought with him that I was more than willing to play my John Malcolm Brinnin to his Dylan Thomas, referring to one of the seminal intersections of professor and poet in the latter's tours to the United States. I have yet to record, though it would be no small matter to do so, the substance of these conversations, and I recall that they cycled through a fairly focused agenda. It should be noted, however, and not parenthetically, that no subject, no commitment to poetry itself, superseded Leo's love for his wife Nancy and daughter Amy. I can't recall, in fact, any conversation in which he didn't invoke their names in the kind of undiluted 1ove he obvious1y had for his special poetic craft.

Leo was always aware of the contemporary artistic scene and could join current references to movies, for example, to a knowledge of a much wider film canon. While he was politically aware and congenitally a supporter of the political Left, he was not driven ideologically. His identification with the have-nots of the larger social order was no idle abstraction for him but a world he knew at first hand. Always at the center of any conversation, of course, was poetry. His comments to us were variations on a number of interviews he gave over the years, which taken as an aggregate produce a genuine personal poetics that found precise focus in his concluding comment in his introduction to *New and Collected Poems* (1989). "I am extremely disturbed by even the conception of an 'official' literature," he begins. "We must insist on imagination, risk, thinking you see something and going for it, letting the poem make itself whatever it wants, free reign to the imagination and heart, or poetry loses a chance just sometimes to achieve greatness. Most of the time we fail. We write more failures than successes but just every once in a while we may succeed."

In a life marked so often by travail, we can see, too, frequent measures of Leo's success—winning the Shelley Memorial prize, placing important volumes at major commercial publishers (an increasing rarity today), being awarded the laureateship of his adopted State of Connecticut and serving as Poet-in-Residence of the Connecticut State University System. In the latter he made a particular contribution, one little known, in bringing poetry to the public schools of Connecticut. He did so particularly at Windham High School where for more than a decade he was a regular visitor to Mary's English classes. In time spent with Leo, Mary may have few peers, and she had the foresight to preserve on tape such visits, thus providing a remarkable record of Leo as a public figure reading and commenting on his own poetry.

A visit on May 27, 1998 is at once typical and instructive as one can see in action Leo's literary persona, which was in fact his essential personality. He sits at the desk at the front of the room; attentive senior students ask sensible questions, which become an occasion for Leo to provide a wide-ranging response that combines literary history (references in a brief period to such figures as Boccaccio, Spenser, Faulkner, Poe, Hemingway, and Swift) and allows him to focus on the creation of his own verse. Here, and on other occasions in Mary's class, Leo presented the genesis of a variety of poems, including "Staten Island Ferry," "The Whole Thing About Jedge's House," and "Scott Huff."

On this particular day, he provided extended commentary on the genesis of what many would argue is his greatest poem, "What Can I Leave for You to Feel of Me." In this text, an almost ideal context for invoking the critical apparatus of the New Historicists, he joins Thaovenhosen's raid on colonial Deerfield, which subsequently led to a brutal diaspora taking inhabitants as far north as Canada, to the final moments of John Sheldon's wife as the sturdy door of her home failed to protect her from axe and rifle. The essential genesis of the poem is, of course, biographical. Leo, in fact, was simply in the Deerfield area hoping to make a sale of typewriter ribbons when a friend suggested they look at the famous Sheldon door. The terrible history suggested by the door, as widely known as it was, needed something else-the transformative power of a great poet who through his verse immortalized not only a terrorized community but also the awful final moments of one of its members. Because of Leo's chance encounter with Deerfield and the poetic eyes with which he constantly surveyed the world, we feel for John Shelton's wife and her larger community in a way never before possible.

While material such as this that we have preserved in our "Leo Connellan File" is special to us and of use to potential biographers and critics, perhaps two items—a photograph and a letter—are particularly special. Leo gave us a photograph taken of him in the White Horse Tavern in New York City in 1950. He is standing next to a young man in an Air Force uniform, dressed himself in a checked sportscoat and a scarf used as a casual cravat. At this time he would have been around twenty-two years old. He gazes at the camera not aware, obviously, of the travail that lay ahead but equally of the great success that would ultimately be his. Yet at that time he was by poetry possessed as he would be throughout his life. The intensity of this commitment is seen some forty years later when on December 21, 1992 he wrote to us: "Christmas is turning out to be *good*! I'm suddenly at work on new poems that I never expected to write. It is silly to say this, but my head swims in music when this comes back." How fortunate we all are that for so many years that Leo's head did "swim in music" and that because of his remarkable talent we can all continue to hear it today.

from *Poetrybay On-Line Poetry Magazine*, Spring 2001

In Memoriam, Leo Connellan

David B. Axelrod

"It's me—Leo. Do you have time to listen? Listen, they just put my work on a website in Maine. I gave my daughter Amy the computer so I can't see it but you can take a look at it. I'm one of the people they picked as Maine's best." It's Leo Connellan on the phone burning my ear. I've known him since the 70's and it's always interesting when Leo calls. Poet Laureate of Connecticut, Poet in Residence for the State University System of Connecticut.

You know, I wish I could hear Leo on the phone again. It was a Thursday evening, February 22, this year. It was daughter Amy who called to tell me Leo had a massive stroke. The body lingered on but soon enough Leo was completely gone. The large physical presence of Leo, that is. Luckily, a very large body of Leo's poetry remains. It's impossible to think of the poetry of Leo Connellan without thinking of the man. That's not a biographical fallacy. Leo's work was deeply personal, torn from the hard-scrabble childhood of Maine's coast. He turned the premature death of parents, the abuse at the hands of those who "cared for him" into a tough American kind of poetry. His views were somewhere between paranoid and cruelly honest. If he observed, it was with a zeal—that part of him that was tough and genuine. Here's a fellow who found his way into the literary world with a salesman's savvy. But Leo was never a con artist; he had the real goods to sell—quality poetry. Leo was no language poet, even as his plain style evoked instant detail. He was not afraid to write longer than most magazines would publish even as he could scalpel a poem down to just the essentials. Readers, with luck, will find more and more of his poems in anthologies.

But it is the man I want to remember here, in ways those who didn't know him might only hear in odd anecdotes. Leo, who could tell a politically incorrect joke with aplomb. Leo who loved his wife Nancy and daughter Amy more than life—so that when he was on booze, with the greatest strength of character, he stopped to stay with them and be a good husband, father, citizen. When he was broke, he'd climb the steps of high-rise buildings with a broom, swallowing his pride and sweeping for a few extra bucks.

Luckily, hard times didn't hound Leo. He persisted even as the Muse stayed steadfastly with him. He got himself a coveted poetry appointment in Connecticut. Fancy-ass poets, stunned by his successes, often tried to leave him out. Hurt as he was, it never affected his creativity. Leo came to poetry later than many of the wonder-boys and girls birthed yearly out of the M.F.A.'s of America. But his quantity and quality are stunning. Look at the links. Look into Leo. If ever there were an adage that would apply as inspiration looking at the life and poetry of Leo Connellan, it would be simply: "Don't let the bastards beat you down." (I miss you Leo. Maybe give me a call....)

from *Connecticut Review*, Spring 2001

An Interview with Leo Connellan

David Bradt

Leo Connellan is Connecticut's second poet laureate and poet in residence of the Connecticut State University System. He is the author of fifteen books of poetry and was the 1982 recipient of the Shelley Memorial Award. The following exchange took place in September of 2000 in Griswold, Connecticut.

Bradt: *Let me ask you about the subjects of your poems. Where do they come from?*

Connellan: In my poems I try to write about what it means to be human. Conflicts of the heart are more interesting and serious than ephemeral topics. I look at a poem by Robert Browning, say, like "Porphyria's Lover" or "My Last Duchess" and I try to see what wasn't said, and perhaps my poem begins there. For example, at first I couldn't understand why he wrote "Porphyria's Lover," because it's about a girl who arrives at a man's house. Obviously they are going to score together, but he knows what she wants to do, and he kills her. He is obviously some kind of upper class male chauvinist who thinks—or knows—that he can get away with it, like the duke in "My Last Duchess." I suddenly realized that a secret of art is to enrage. Jonathan Swift wanted to suggest cooking the Irish babies just so I'd get mad. And perhaps Browning wrote "Porphyria's Lover" or "My Last Duchess" so I'd be outraged at his presumption. This is where I think writing begins, with an attempt to outrage the reader. Or at least to cause some kind of emotional response, because that's what I think the job is.

Bradt: *When in the process of writing a poem does the shape of the poem on the page suggest itself to you?*

Connellan: I don't know the answer to that, but I'll tell you the best I can. When something occurs to me, I know I'm going to have to work. I write it all out, and then I use what I call my cookie cutter, to cut it as much as I can, and when it's cut as much as I can, it starts to take shape. When that happens I can begin to visualize it on the page the way I want it to look. It's a mysterious process that I don't fully understand myself.

Bradt: *What are your writing habits, if you have any? Do you have a schedule of some sort?*

Connellan: I've had to work all my life. I was Eastern regional sales manager for a large manufacturer of stationery supplies. I had one child. I have been getting up at 3:30 in the morning for fifty years. I have learned, don't overdo it, but do it a certain amount of time. Four to six, I write. And I carried my writing with me in my sales bag, or now in my brief case when I teach, and when I have a break, I read it. If it strikes me in the face, I keep it. If it doesn't, I get rid of it. Because if it doesn't slap me, it definitely isn't going to slap that unknown person, my reader.

It's up to the writer. Writers are human beings. James Baldwin told me he couldn't start before ten o'clock at night, so he wrote from ten until five o'clock in the morning, and you wouldn't see Jimmy until about two in the afternoon. It's been a practical matter for me. I have to make a living, and that living has been as a salesman or sales manager, or now, as a teacher. I could find excuses—papers, homework—but I get up at three in the morning, go downstairs and put the coffee pot on, and between four and six, when nobody's awake, I write. Then I've done today what I want to do, before I do what others want me to do. It's a commitment. There's no excuse in the ballgame I'm talking about. Maybe people will think you're not a writer or not know you are, but if you're a writer you're writing. You hear all sorts of excuses. I was at one of the universities when I first came to Connecticut, and one of the English department professors said, "Leo, you mustn't be offended if the staff doesn't seem to do more than nod at you. If they weren't busy teaching classes they would write poetry so much better than yours." I looked at him and said, "I guess a bird in the hand is worth two in the bush," because I didn't know what else to say to him.

Bradt: *Your style has been described as "colloquial" and "realistic." What does that mean to you?*

Connellan: I'm not sure. But maybe it means I don't imitate others, or that I'm not an "academic" poet. I made a film for Maine Public Television and somebody said, "Leo, we've got to ask this: What do you think makes you unique?" My answer was, "Unique will be in later. I'm just Leo." I think I listen with my middle ear. You tell me a story or one is told to me, and I try to invent my poems so they sound as if someone is talking to you, and I try to make them seem simple. Let me tell you about one of the greatest compliments I've ever had in my life. I was still young, and had been invited to give a reading at the University of Maine in South Portland. A young woman on the faculty apparently did not want me invited—and that's all right; no one has to love me. But she bothered to come to the reading with the rest of the faculty, and when they got there, she stood up to leave, and everyone looked at her, and she said, "I don't know why they say he's any good. I don't have any trouble understanding him." And I wanted to get down and thank God for all those hours of work, because to me, you write it all down, then you edit it, then you shape it and you take your reader into consideration. You assume that reader knows exactly what you mean. But you don't know what a reader knows. Somebody hands you the ball and you just throw the ball. And you let the guys in the stands decide if you're any good.

Bradt: *How many revisions would you say a typical poem goes through?*

Connellan: The poem is done when it's done. For example, the trilogy, *The Clear Blue Lobster-Water Country* took me ten years. The night my daughter was born I was in such a high creative mode I wrote a poem in one shot. That has happened seldom—maybe once more in my life. As a writer, I'm like a boxer. I know what I'm going to do to throw a punch to the jaw, and after awhile, if the poem is finished, I never touch it again. That's what I'm going to live with. Hemingway once said, "It's never what you had done, but always what you could do." The hardest thing for human beings to do is to commit themselves, and to say, "This is finished and I'm going to give it to you. I don't care what you think of it. You don't have to like it, but it's finished." It takes maturity, it takes work, it takes thinking.

It takes the maturity to know when to say, "This is it. Good, bad or indifferent, this is it." And it takes learning. I think this is what some of the young people who go to poetry slams and wiggle their butts do not realize. First of all, they need to show that they understand allusion, that even if you don't like what you read, you understand where it came from.

I'm seventy-two years old and I've been writing since 1946. Somebody said, "Who did you study with?" and I said, "I studied with Leo Connellan." What I mean is, in the beginning I said to myself, I want to read twentieth century poets, but I also want to read poems that have held up for five hundred years. I don't care whose translation. If it's lasted this long, what is it about the poem that makes me want to read it. What I've tried to get into my work is what would make it last. You may not like it—but you read the work and you say, maybe it will last...

There are a lot of writers who were not popular. They said that Ezra Pound was fascist and a Nazi and had to save his life. But you can't get by the brilliance of his work. So I try to imagine what I should do, and I could be wrong as well as right. But at least I've done what I could do to write my work, knowing that I'm going to fail. Shakespeare and Donne and Browning and Poe and Emily Dickinson have come before me. So what's the job to do? The job's to be the best Leo Connellan I can be, and I let somebody else decide whether it's good or not.

Bradt: *All poets are influenced by others. Who were the poets that influenced your early work?*

Connellan: Robert Frost. You can't get by him. People tell me he was a terrible man. I don't care about personality or sex or church. You cannot get by Frost. He forces you to commit yourself. You read "Two Tramps in Mud Time," and he makes you make a decision about it. Federico Garcia Lorca in his "Lament for Ignazio Sanchez Mejia." In America, Karl Shapiro—the sound and music in the language, the rhythm. Many of the poets I like are totally unlike me. I could never be a genius like W. H. Auden, but I can learn from him. Or Delmore Schwartz. You can't get by Poe, either.

People ask me if I believe in God, and I don't know what they mean. But I say, "God gave us Mozart and Beethoven and Picasso. And he gave us Michelangelo and Emily Dickinson, and he gave us Poe too." When you read Poe, you realize your frailties, and it frees you to try to write your own work, because you know before you start you're no good and you're never going to be any good. But you try to be the best "you" you might become.

Bradt: *In your official capacities as writer in residence and poet laureate, you spend a good deal of time with young people. What is your approach to poetry with them?*

Connellan: When I'm in a classroom with young people they often say, "I don't understand this poetry stuff." When this happened recently, I slapped my thigh three times, hard, and said, "Don't you think that hurt? Then don't tell me you don't know how to imagine. You saw me do this and you imagined how it hurt. You are as capable of understanding poetry as anybody else." Or I ask them, What is an assassin? Somebody who kills somebody. What does an assassin look like? Like anybody. Imagine if someone knocked on the classroom door, and he had a mailman's uniform on, should we be courteous enough to say, "Excuse me, this is a classroom, you'll have to go to the office with the mail," and if he pulled a weapon and shot the janitor, what does that make him? He is the assassin hidden within who you thought he was. When I can get young people to understand how the imagination works, then they can begin to understand and appreciate poetry.

Bradt: *Did you choose poetry, or did poetry choose you? Was there an epiphany of some kind when you knew you were a poet?*

Connellan: I guess poetry found me. My mother died when I was seven years of age, and I was a kind of dreamer at Rockland High School. One day, after we'd read Joyce Kilmer's "Trees," Mrs. Ludwig, our teacher, asked us to put a leaf on Joyce Kilmer's tree. And I wrote the poem "The Leaf" when I was sixteen years old. Unknown to anybody, she sent it to *Scholastic Scope*, the national High School Poetry Association magazine, and it won first prize. I saw the prize in the school library with Edna St.Vincent Millay and the basketball and football trophies, and I just never wanted to do anything else. But it took me from 1946 to 1974 to get a book published, and I also had my theories about publishing poetry in magazines and journals, but that's something else.

Bradt: *Poets are often romanticized as loners working in ivory towers. What is the reality of your experience as a poet?*

Connellan: I think that's crap. Let me tell you what I mean. Some teachers and college professors have a secure tenure, and they have days off, and so do I. So when someone talks about an ivory tower, what they're trying to say is, "I don't have to do what he has to do. I don't have to make room for my writing." But you can't make the excuses. When you have the free time, you can go to a softball game, or the poolroom, or for a beer, or you can write. Sometimes, when they find out you choose to write, they resent you. I don't want you to think I'm paranoid, but I'm not. I'm Leo. But I know paranoid. People look at me and say I don't look like William Holden or Harrison Ford—that I don't look like a writer. I write because it's what I can't help myself from trying to do, but if you're any good at it, you know right from the word "go" there is no "separate peace." Hemingway knew that very clearly when he wrote "Up in Michigan." Nobody sent for me. Nobody cares much if I'm here. Only I care. So I think the secret of writing is the writer cares and is willing to bloody his nose. And every once in awhile I will meet a real writer, who will know that I'm a guy who does his business and doesn't try to toady up to anyone. So many people have reasons for not wanting to do it. The literary world is full of poetry magazines and anthologies, edited by third-rate people. If they accept your poems, that's not necessarily the best you've written, so you learn to live without them. But you have to live with that. Some writers want it too fast. They want to be known, but you have to have something to say. And you have to do the work, instead of going to the softball game, or the poolroom, or for a beer.

Bradt: *Many writers look upon writing as therapy. Is that a view you share?*

Connellan: No. I see writing as something you have to do if you're a writer. You can't help yourself from doing it because believe me, if I could stop, I would. Think of Pete Sampras, the tennis player. He's got forty million dollars. Why does he keep playing? Because he can't help it. I think that people who sing or write can't help doing it. If they could, they wouldn't. It takes time; it saps your emotions. You have to look not at what others think is true, but what you think is true, and to seduce the reader into your point of view—or into a point of view. Let me give you an example. I haven't lived in Maine for thirty-five years, but I know the truth of the place. I wrote a poem called "Fair Warning." When, in the state of Maine, you rent a cottage, the state is greedy for your money, so they will sell you a license to lobster. Now you can go from your rented cottage straight out and catch lobsters. If you take them straight back in, you can cook them, and you can even invite me to dinner. But if I reach into my pocket for money to buy them, I'll be lucky if I don't get my head blown off, because this is how those people make their living. So you have to be able to show that point of view, to make readers not offended by what they read but understand that the writer is stating what he thinks he has observed, and I can either agree or disagree. But I can't say it's not writing, he hasn't made an argument. So you try to write, free of everyone you will ever meet, hoping you will find a central core that everyone will look at and say, "Yes, I see what the guy means." Let me show you:

Down the dark Pine green,
in deep blue quiet, the
flippers of sea waves
slapping inches off the shore.
Scent of deer moss and fern
soured, all the silence shattered
by the abrupt dog bark of gun blast
rapping the knuckles of water
that lets a stranger's boat lie bobbing
and the foreigner lobstering!

Take my virgin daughter if
I don't kick your teeth out,
take my worn out woman
skinny on my provision,
but threaten our living, thief
in my salt flowing refrigerator,
I'll take your life.

I tried to write something so that if you'd never met Leo Connellan, you could understand what I mean about a particular way of life in Maine.

Bradt: *Your poems often focus on working class people and the disadvantaged. How do you explain your choice of subject matter?*

Connellan: Because I came from the Depression years. My father was a lawyer. But in the Depression, nobody had money for a lawyer. So while we were never really destitute, there were times when all that was in the icebox was a can of Franco-American spaghetti. I used to make a joke and say that I gave my brother Jimmy the spaghetti, and I ate the can. My father was a middle class survivor who was postmaster of Rockland, Maine. Most of the people I knew were struggling, but they had no voice. So I wrote what I thought came naturally to me.

I was at the University of Maine a few years ago, reading as a visiting writer, and Dr. Hatlen, a professor there, has a rule. If you take his class, you have to go and listen to all the visiting writers. I read my poem "By the Blue Sea," which makes the point that the only reason the boy—who thinks he's really something—ever got anything from the girl is because she gave it to him. At the end of the reading, a girl leaped across chairs and called to me. She said, "I only came here today because Dr. Hatlen requires you to. But I'm glad I came because that poem is about me." Here was a girl, an unknown person, who knew what I read.

I'm not an academic, so I'm not out to show that I'm accomplished in language, but rather that I can create an image that you can recognize, and I try to write about the people I knew when I was young, when I hitchhiked the United States and panhandled and hoboed. I met decent, good people who were out of work. I met them at places like the Salvation Army.

Bradt: *Do your concerns for the underprivileged lead to political statements? Do you take political stands on issues?*

Connellan: Not consciously, though maybe my poems seem somewhat political. I'm not a politician and I'm not a joiner. I just try to do honest work that ordinary people can relate to. In the twentieth century we've had a lot of gimmicks and people trying to astonish and outrage us. And we live in a culture that seems frightened not to enjoy being outraged. In my own family I was nobody until I began to be noticed. Until the poetry prizes came along, and until I became poet laureate and writer-in-residence for the university system, I didn't have anything to point to with dignity. You learn to live without it.

But I've had many friends who have helped me. Richard Selzer is a close friend. Sydney Lea, a distinguished scholar and teacher. Richard Eberhart gave me my break. Richard Wilbur and Robert Penn Warren are two others who helped me. Nobody does it by themselves. Anybody who thinks so is delusional. You may be James Joyce or J. D. Salinger and do your work by yourself. But if you get anywhere with it, it's because other people admire what you try to do, and they help you in any way they can.

Bradt: *Why does poetry matter?*

Connellan: Poetry matters because people can join the poem, bring their experience to the poem. Poetry creates an image that depends on the reader's looking at it to be successful, whereas a story tells it. You really don't have as much choice of interpretation. Nathaniel Hawthorne wrote a story called "The Minister's Black Veil" about Handkerchief Moody in York, Maine. You understand what he's doing, but you don't have a say in it. As a reader you don't have any input. But with poetry, if the poet is good, you do. Each of us, like the writer F. Scott Fitzgerald said, is many people. If he is any good, the poet creates imagery that allows you to come to it through your experience, your knowledge. Poetry allows you to do this and be part of the poem. It is the form of art for everyone.

Bradt: *You're a teacher. If you had young students with some writing talent, and if you decided to help them as others have helped you, what advice would you give them?*

Connellan: To read as much as they can. Then find who you are. Don't imitate. Read others to find out what makes them good. Then take the next step. I might give them a list of people to read because they have lasted. And look at the literary journals to find ones that are receptive to their kinds of writing, and submit to them. And to be ready for rejection. Don't live your life to get published; the credentials you get will not be as important as writing the poem. Your work will bring you recognition or nothing will. As Wesley McNair has said, we have to honor and admire writers who stayed in the game and did the work.

A Few Last Words For Leo

Harry Brody

It's been a couple years since I got the call from Amy, Leo's daughter, that Boppledock went down and, this once, stayed on the mat.

Although our formerly furious communiqués over the horn had, of late, fallen to a trickle, as I'd become distracted by my day-job, defending death-row inmates, and Leo had reached recognition, and some semblance of security, with his Laureate-ship, I couldn't imagine Leo actually dying.

Nevermind his relentless maladies of mind and spirit and the real and imagined enemies natural to an artist so passionately affixed to the heart-root of the American spirit, to the en-poemed people he gave majestic voice to, and to the continual, relentless making of his high and hard-won art, my friend of twenty years, of the countless letters, calls, and even a vacation visit to our sullen hut in the alien South, had been silenced....

Hung up. Went to the bookcase. Pulled down the poems.
The poems!

I think of Leo in the line of E.A. Robinson, and Hart Crane, his work being no less elegantly crafted of the common tongue at its most elegantly agile. In a time of two-bit Bukowski's on the one hand and marble-ized, Medici would-be's on the other, Leo Connellan always insisted on speaking American with the dignity of Good Book prophecy, with the gravity of a deeply held and joyful sense of justice the hacks lacked and the high-hats scoffed at, and with an almost Brucian ethnic delight that honors honest laughter and, billowing the sails full speed ahead, keeps the worship of remorse in check. Savage in his dedication to this work, he wrote small lives large enough to last.

Leo Connellan's accomplishment will become increasingly clear as the winnowing continues. We can say this though: his briefer lyrics ("Look at lakes, now shattered mirrors meld") happily marry Whitman's spirit to Dickinson's density, safely bearing Beauty's shell-borne body to the shore, and his longer work, uniquely imagined in a time of timid ambitions and book-tour inanity, particularly his trilogy, which, with *The Bridge and Leaves*, fulfills a larger American trilogy, finally reconciles Emily's inner weather with Walt's expansive territorial visions, ancestries and agon which had seemed, for a century, to cross America on parallel plains through a nothing prairie night in which the fry cook's smoke-rings halo Hank Williams' lonesome whistle wafting weepishly from the dash of Kerouac's stolen Chevrolet.

As every intersection is a cross, Death will have the body, but, by the Life of Leo's voice, now lion-throated, now nightingale-numinous, sounding such wild imaginings as ever the chisel has convinced stone of, It cannot rive, from the perpetuity of papyrus, the perpetuating tongue which, Ezra, does remain, amended by Connellan, blazingly American in its heart-broke salutations.

from *Connecticut Review*, Spring 2003

Leo Connellan—"Unique Will Come Later; I'm Leo"

Gary Carlson

If Arthur Miller had chosen to make his tragic hero Willy Loman a poet instead of a traveling salesman, chances are, Willy probably would have resembled Leo Connellan. Flop-eared and jowly, with cowlicky white hair, an unfashionably wide tie drawn open at the neck of his wrinkled shirt, and a pair of blue slacks worn about as high as they can go, Leo certainly looked the part of a latter-day Willy Loman. As a matter of fact, during the 70's and 80's Leo put in time and logged countless miles as a traveling salesman—of typewriter ribbons produced by a company that refused to believe the age of the typewriter was coming to an end. If that's not tragically Loman-esque, then I don't know what is. And Leo Connellan's life—all 72 years of it—was too often a repository for such bitter ironies, cruel jokes, disappoints, and failures. Yet unlike Miller's Loman, Leo survived. More than that, he triumphed. For unlike Willy, who eventually succumbed to the bankruptcy and hypocrisy of his own dreams, Leo Connellan spent most of his adult life honoring the truth by clinging tenaciously, even courageously, to the one thing that always sustained him—his poetry.

Poet Laureate of Connecticut and Poet-in-Residence for the Connecticut State University System, winner of the prestigious Shelley Memorial Award, and author of fifteen acclaimed books of poetry, after a hardscrabble, often demeaning life of sacrificing all for his art, before his untimely death in 2001, Leo Connellan, the ultimate Survivor-Poet, had at long last begun to receive the kind of recognition and regard that many of his fellow poets had accorded him for years:

> "Everybody interested in modern poetry should read the passionate work of Leo Connellan . . . whose textbook is raw life and whose words can be understood by anyone."
>
> —Richard Eberhart

> "Connellan's poems are vivid, harsh, spare, surely cadenced and colloquially eloquent. There is no poet quite like him."
>
> —Richard Wilbur

> "[Connellan's] poems are a celebration of sorts, a celebration of survival by a heart that has prevailed."
>
> —Hubert Selby

Born in Portland, Maine, in November of 1928, Leo's boyhood was a far cry from the kind of bucolic, idyllic "Downeast" memoirs one might find in the pages of *Yankee* magazine. "It was the Depression, and the people scowled at you most of the time," Leo recalled during an October, 2000 interview at Norwalk Community College, where he was appearing as Keynote Speaker for their First Annual Connecticut Writers' Conference. "They mimicked you, wanted you to fail. They were isolated, insulated people, distrustful of anyone or anything that was different."

In those days, in a land of lumberjacks and lobstermen, Leo Connellan—a boy who at the age of 15 decided he wanted to be a poet—must have indeed attracted more than his share of abuse and suspicion. "A teacher of mine in high school read Joyce Kilmer's poem "The Tree" and asked us to 'add a leaf' to her 'tree.' I did, and I won a prize—which the teacher put up right next to the football trophies. From that moment on, I never wanted to do anything else." However, for a budding young poet-in-the-making, there was little understanding or encouragement to be found in Portland—or anywhere else in the working-class, ultra-patriotic, America-at-war of 1942. Yet Leo continued to live in Maine, absorbing the sights, the sounds, the language and way-of-life of a place and people that would always regard him as alien—and haunt him for the rest of his life.

"I finally left when my father made it quite clear that he wouldn't stand for me being a poet. So I took off. I was 23. I hoboed around, hitch-hiked through 41 states. Worked at odd jobs, pumping gas, washing dishes, unloading freight, and cooking. I was a good cook—which is useful. A good cook can always get a job. I also learned the importance of honesty. If I came into a place and asked for a job, I'd tell him, 'I'm only gonna be here for two weeks, but I'll work hard, I'll show up on time, and I won't steal from the till.' And I'd get hired, because they could recognize the truth when they heard it—could see it in my eyes."

Leo lived like this for a number of years, existing "in dirty, rancid apartments" and drinking too much—a problem that would persist and eventually grow unmanageable. "Writers were expected to drink back then—so it was easy to fall into that trap. And there were times, back then and later, when I gave up writing and just drank. But never for long. I just couldn't stop writing."

At the age of 27, Leo briefly returned to Maine. However, knowing that his family and neighbors viewed his failed life with equal measures of pleasure and contempt, he didn't stay long.

In 1961, in New York City, he met his wife Nancy, the love of his life—the one thing in his life, besides poetry, that remained constant, nourishing and sustaining him. Originally from Berkeley, she was a social worker willing to support her husband, if necessary, to allow him to write. They remained together for over 40 years and raised a daughter, Amy Charlotte. In 1965, Leo finally had his first publication. He was 37 years old. His first book wouldn't be published for almost another decade, in 1974. "I didn't allow myself to become the victim of editors," Leo explained, referring to his long, difficult apprenticeship. Unwilling to compromise his art, he instead fought to have his work published just as he wrote it. "You do the work, you stay invisible, and if the work is good, people will eventually find you." Too many writers, he felt, lose faith in themselves. They fall into the trap of celebrity, of currying favor with whatever literary crowd is in fashion, and then writing for them and only them. And while the benefits of appealing to the "in-crowd" can include the kind of publication, awards, and appointments that make for successful literary careers, too often the artist ends up sacrificing his or her "soul"—and losing whatever truly makes one an artist, as opposed to a poseur.

"I was interviewed on TV once," Leo said in his typically whiny, naturally cranky voice, his soft mouth twisted into a sort of half-smile, his sad, pale blue eyes—so often filled with need and the knowledge of pain and loss—momentarily glinting with delight. "I was asked what I thought made me 'unique' among modern writers. '"Unique" will come later,' I told him; 'I'm Leo.'" Enjoying his own story, Leo laughed, loud and hard. But as the laughter subsided, he grew serious and talked in careful, measured sentences.

"Let me tell you—there are barracudas out there, people who are out to get you. But you persist. You call people. You send your stuff out. You meet with people. You realize that everything is politics. You realize that if something good happens to a writer, it's usually because it benefits somebody else. So you go out and you promote yourself. I had to fight to get published. And that is what you must do—every day. You work at your job to put bread in your mouth, but first you get up at 3:30 every morning and write from 4-6. Then you put it in your briefcase and you take it to work. You look at it during the day, and if it still slaps you in the face, then maybe you work on it some more; maybe you even keep it. But you learn that everything you write is not gold." Especially, he cautioned, when writing under the influence.

Always a hard drinker, it finally took its toll on Leo in the mid-to late-70's. "It ruined the work," Leo said matter-of-factly. "Read my early work and you can see how it affected the work. I knew I had to stop, but I was afraid. I was afraid that quitting would kill me—that my heart would literally burst. But that's how you beat addiction—by making up your mind to die. I knew my heart would explode if I stopped drinking. But I stopped anyway. I went through the shakes that make you wish for death. I faced my worst fear—and overcame it."

The wages of that struggle showed plainly in every line of Leo's ravaged face. And there was more to come. In 1982, the typewriter ribbon company he worked for finally went out of business. Leo was 48 years old. "We lost our house, everything. I had to scramble around, substitute teaching. I did what I could. My wife worked hard to support us. It was tough, but I never stopped writing."

Then, that same year ('82), something totally unexpected occurred. The Poetry Society of America selected Leo's book *Shatterhouse* for its

Shelley Memorial Award—a moment in his life that he often singled out as the happiest and most satisfying. "Maybe I'm no good—but I'm the best that Leo Connellan has it in him to be," and he was never afraid to say how satisfying it was to see that simple fact publicly acknowledged and lauded.

And what exactly was Leo Connellan, poet? "Like Lorca, I believe in the power of metaphor. Lorca always handled it so beautifully, so delicately. 'The lovers have become photographs.' "Her thighs escape me/like two silver fish.' You don't see language used that way today. Metaphor is a lost art. Now you have people who put on their 'writing clothes' and wiggle their asses and slam their poetry—but are they poets? I worked for 30 years to make my poems seem effortless—figuring a way of inverting the poem, as if I'm giving the poem back to you. Then you have someone come up to you who always intended to write but never did, and they resent you. They've opted for the safe jobs and paid vacations and their dreams of the writers they could have been, and when they see you they're disappointed. They want you to look and sound like the poet they know they could have been if only. And there's resentment there, because I don't fit that image, so therefore I must not be much of a poet. I once heard someone complain, 'He's not so good. I understood every word he said.'"

Till the day he died Leo believed that writers must be willing to risk that kind of resentment, even anger, if they are ever to achieve their own voices. "My poems don't preach, but they're not just flat statements of fact. That's not art. You must create it on the page—the thing itself, an image powerful enough for the reader to recognize it as true—however unpleasant or difficult it may be. It's in that power of recognition that we rise above the mundane, the brutal, the horribly familiar, and truly see. This is how I deal with horror—whether it's my own personal horror or the holocaust—I seek to give the victims of this world a hook to hang their hope on.

"I also have tried to move a step beyond the writers whose work I admire—Swift, Spender, Browning, St. Vincent Millay, Frost, Shapiro. They presented but usually drew no conclusion. I observe, I present, but I also engage, I enrage, I want them to act—to draw some conclusion."

The pain that caused his face to flush and his voice to strain as he struggled to make himself understood was disconcerting, to say the least. Seventy-two-year-olds are not supposed to be this passionate about anything, much less poetry. "Look at me! Are you listening to me?" he would demand as I struggled to keep up with his stream of words. But then, to Leo Connellan, poetry was life and death itself—never to be taken lightly or for granted, always demanding our full attention.

Having struggled so very long, throughout his life, to be a poet, to beat his addiction to drink, to ultimately be recognized for what he achieved through his art, toward the end of his life, Leo Connellan certainly appeared to have finally conquered all his fears. Yet one remained—haunting him, driving him for as long as his brave heart continued to beat.

"I don't want to lose my talent. I want to keep writing," he said, almost desperately, that cool, autumn morning in NCC's East Campus Lounge, a crooked smile lingering on his ravaged face. "Maybe I'll get that MacArthur Grant, that Pulitzer. Who knows? Still," he sighed, "although prizes are the meal ticket, you write anyway. Hoping you'll be published. Hoping you'll be read."

He leaned back in his chair, his hands locked behind his unkempt white head of hair, his glasses resting crookedly on his milkdrop nose. We'd been talking for over two hours now, and Leo showed no signs of tiring. Instead, he looked straight into my eyes—fiercely, defiantly proud, yet calm as only a man who knew himself and was reconciled to this world could be. "It's always been a struggle," he said. "And maybe I haven't won that Pulitzer. But I have the poems—enough for me to live on, anyway. And that's all I ever really wanted."

Author's note:
My interview with Leo took place in October of 2000, just a few weeks before his gracious appearance at the very first Connecticut Writers' Conference, which I had organized on behalf of Norwalk Community College. Leo was one of the stars of the Conference and

thoroughly enjoyed himself, reading his work to a large crowd, participating in several panel discussions, and hob-nobbing with the many writers and students who participated in the day.

I showed Leo a finished draft of this article later that year, and he gave it his blessing. We stayed in touch, talking about the next year's Conference. Unfortunately, he never made that Conference, due to his untimely death in February of 2001. We all lost a great artist and a great friend on that day.

I offer this article as my tribute to a man I was fortunate to have as a teacher, a mentor, and a friend. Leo, we'll never forget you.

from *Maine Times*, November 1 1999

Review of *The Maine Poems*

William Carpenter

I was walking down Rockland's main drag one evening, back in the seventies, when a biker rode his Harley right up on the sidewalk, into the lobby of the elegant old Thorndike Hotel and up to the registration desk. He stayed right astride her, idling, while he registered for his room. That's the kind of town Rockland once was, coastal refinement and semi-urban squalor, melting-pot ethnicity and a wide-open outlaw reputation. It was also a center of creative vitality that spawned Walter Piston and Kosti Ruohomaa and Louise Nevelson, as well as one of the strongest voices in Maine poetry, Leo Connellan.

Connellan is the James Joyce of Maine. Though he has lived away for his whole writing career, he has re-created Rockland as the "Lime City" of his imagination. It is the working-class heartland to which he returns in every poem, whether as hormone-ridden street kid or visiting poet in disguise. Like the homesick nightly dreams of the traveler, every one of these poems is a vehicle for the exiled Connellan to pound on the door of an old girlfriend or high school buddy and reminisce or get drunk or get in a fight or get laid.

Alas, there's no new work in this volume for the Connellan fan. The poems are mostly selected and reprinted from his 1989 *New and Collected Poems*, with just three taken from books of the nineties. However, because the 1989 book has gone out of print, Blackberry Press has done Maine literature a great service by re-issuing these twenty-six poems, the best of his Maine work with the exception of the prize-winning *Clear Blue Lobster-Water Country*.

Though they often portray the stark, post-depression Maine of Leo's boyhood, they were written in the sixties and seventies, the "confessional" period of American poetry. They are simultaneously portraits and self-portraits. The exiled poet weaves his own secret remembered life into the austere, often tragic lives of his Rockland characters. These are homecoming fantasies of relentless nostalgia and unredeemable guilt. True to the confessional mode, the poet lets you in on his dark secrets: alcoholism, sexual irresponsibility, a behavioral "sneakiness" which often left someone else to pick up the pieces.

Connellan has a wonderful explanation of creativity, quoted in Sandy Phippen's preface: "Either we are born brilliant or something disturbs us." In Connellan's case both may be true. He lost his mother when he was a young boy, a "disturbance" that produced an irremediable sense of solitude and abandonment. His answer was to abandon his native town, then to express his love for it in all his work. Connellan's poetry is obsessed with this paradox: the cruelty of departure and the impossibility of ever getting away.

They are all mirrors, these powerful portraits of working-class Rocklanders up against a tough environment in their dead-end lives. The eternal Maine occupations—blueberrying, fishing, quarrying, factory labor, are interchangeable with the poet's own piecework labors. Foremost of his symbols is the lobster. In his long first-person narrative, "Lobster Claw,"—surely the king of all Maine lobster poems—lobster, lobsterman and poet become faces of the same mutual entrapment. With the same desperate hope, the writer lowers a pot into his own sea:

> Lobster, colored
> blue green, sky blue
> bright red, and even
> albino, I'll find you.

Leo Connellan stands out among contemporary Maine poets as one who has been here from birth and knows what lurks beneath the mythos and romance. From "pisspot aristocracy" to the "blood night of chaotic poverty," he takes a scalpel to the Maine class structure in general and, in particular, the edgy nature of sex and gender relations in an fishing environment where killing and blood are the daily facts of life. Maine love can be indifferent and cruel, "the fish lust of your carcass," but also hilarious. Maine men "love their women like a bicycle Tire Pump is loved." They enjoy lust in the snow, "leaving a shape like the two halves of a pear." They have long-term married sex with their eyes closed dreaming of movie stars. They revel in Rockland hotel-room orgies and backwoods gangbangs with a background of Glenn Miller tunes: "A girl I took as a toothpick youth/ with all my blood rushed into my telephone pole...."

An insider who never left the state could not get a perspective on this life. An outsider would never be allowed to see it. To write these poems Connellan has had to maintain a calculated distance between the poles of exile and home, each figured as a kind of death. Maine death takes the form of an ominous, Hitchcock-like flock of sea gulls waiting for "the end I feel is mine in your throat." Death away from home is impersonal, random, "probably in a hallway when my heart finally explodes." Life must be led between them.

Connellan's virtuoso performances are the long portrait narratives like "Edwin Coombs" "Amelia, the Mrs. Brooks of My Childhood," and "By the Blue Sea." Their inclusive human sympathy, New England cadence and narrative drive cast their spell whether you're lucky enough to hear the poet read them or use your auditory imagination on the printed page. But my discoveries this time around were the smaller, quieter poems, the chamber pieces of his work, like "Garbage Trucks," "Shadows," "Blueberry Boy," and "From Five Islands Maine Rocks" with its subtle references to the upriver presence of Maine Yankee. In one of these, "Out Jim Moore's Window," he gives a Frost-like explanation of his lifetime away from home: "Yet back across Kittery bridge/ Things to do still must be/ And I can't come home until they're done."

As readers, we hope the "things to do" are more Maine poems of this caliber, and, if the poet has to go back to Connecticut to write them, we'll let him go.

Apart from Sandy Phippen's glowing and informative preface, the editing of this collection is not up to the standard of the poems. Readers unfamiliar with Leo Connellan's work could be seriously misled by the absence of dates and acknowledgments, giving the impression that the poems are new. Moreover, as I compared this text with the originals, I found numerous misprints throughout the book which made several important passages seem incoherent. Editorial reliance on the spell-check program led to repeating and omitting words, as well as printing "mind" for "mine," "feet" for "feel," "some" for "come," "eyes" for "eye," "an" for "and," "severs Mass" for "serves Mass." Since Leo Connellan's poems ought to be in every bookshelf of Maine literature, I'm confident it will have a second printing in which the errors can be corrected. These poems deserve the highest production standards, since they are, as Leo's buddy Otto Fishinfolk would say, the finest kind.

from *Parnassus Poetry in Review*, 1990

Excerpt from "Narrative Anyone?"

Hayden Carruth

.... Another long poem I have returned to often—four times since it was published in 1985 and before then as the separate parts came out—is Leo Connellan's trilogy, *The Clear Blue Lobster-Water Country*. It is a Modernist poem in some respects. Its structure is random in appearance (though one knows it wasn't in composition), and its mode is lyrical persuasion. But it has a clear narrative content. In large part this content is autobiographical, or at least one assumes it is, but at the same time it has been fictionalized to such an extent that one can't tell where fiction leaves off and autobiography begins. Book One, "Coming to Cummington to Take Kelly," is the story of a trip to Cummington, Mass., where the poet Richard Wilbur lives, to seek a Kelly or Kelley who is mentioned in a poem by Wilbur and who may or may not be a person from the protagonist's childhood. Book Two, "Shatterhouse," is about a sojourn in a drying-out facility. Book Three, "The Clear Blue Lobster -Water Country," begins and ends with the protagonist, now working as a member of a peace group in an unspecified Latin American country, captured there by guerrillas and then rescued, while the central episodes return by flashback to the breakup of the protagonist's family during his childhood in the 1920s and 1930s in Portsmouth, Maine, and elsewhere. I say protagonist as if this weren't Connellan, but clearly, at least in these narratives of the past, it is. In the poem he is called Boppledock or Bop. His language is from the bop era in American culture, urban and hip, full of nervous rhythms—I know nothing quite like it in American poetry. This excerpt is from the stopover in Shatterhouse, which is otherwise known as Little Hope:

> Thinking this, deciding this excited
>
> Toothpick In Featherhat The Farter and
> Blud-geon like aggression, sometimes...how
> you goin't' feel gooud-n-enjoy whut y'do

t'someone you know, make 'em do 'less you
know whut it feel like an 'so no one in
Th'Thrillers motorcycle gang or th'Fierce- White
Bike Company c'd ever say, Bludgeon he "do it"
but couldn't "take it! "...only thang y'caint "take"
is bein' murdered ahaha! Yippie! Bludgeon he
snuck to liquor store and now in "Group"
Lucy Bubblegum looking at Bop and beautiful

tiny Irish lady with vomit in her bland head....

Most of the poem is not in dialect, however. This is from Book One:

Yet in a Nursing home you
gave up a couple of skid row
wine blasts to get him in
away from those awful ones
with squirrels running intimately
up the arm of Smilin' Billy now
he's got strokes, you sat with him
alone by his bed in the dark
hospital room and put your
hand in his hand and
he knew you....

What has always characterized Leo Connellan's work is his refusal of the oracular. In its ordinary sense Modernism has been, without arguing the term, elitist. It just has been. And it is. I've defended it often enough to be able to say this now. It has been internationalist also, and this in spite of the insistence of Williams and his followers on an "American language" and American themes; one cannot read *Paterson* without seeing its affinities not only with Pound, the expatriate, but with, e.g., Cocteau, the Frenchman.

Internationalism and elitism have always gone hand in hand in the American arts. Connellan has resolutely distanced himself from this, while at the same time and just as resolutely he has denied any affiliation with prairie sentimentalism or proletarian utilitarianism. He is a poet of the American working class who is as sophisticated as any of the elite but who has retained working-class values as the nucleus of his program. He is close to Thomas McGrath in this, though his locus is the East Coast, the port towns of New England, Manhattan, not McGrath's midwestern farming environment. Some of Connellan's best poetry before his trilogy was in the collection titled *Another Poet in New York*, in which he experimented with his bop-like prosody and scathing critical attitudes in an urban setting and in which he acknowledged his debt to Lorca. All of Connellan's poetry, including the trilogy, is now available in his *New and Collected Poems*, published last year [1989], certainly one of the liveliest, most accomplished books of poetry we've had recently. Like McGrath's work, however, Connellan's has not been much acknowledged by the Modernist critical establishment—elitist, internationalist, Vendlerist—until now. I hope this will change....

Eulogy delivered at St. Patrick's Cathedral, Norwich, Connecticut, February 26, 2001

LEO CONNELLAN: THE ROCK UPON WHOM WE BUILT THE YOUNG WRITERS PROGRAM

William J. Cibes, Jr.

Leo Connellan is a state treasure. For two states: Connecticut and Maine. Leo Connellan is a state treasure because his poetry will live on in the minds and thoughts of those who read it. Leo is a state treasure because his commitment to writing will live on—in the lives and in the stories and poems of the young writers he has mentored.

Leo Connellan wrote his poems because he wanted to be a writer. "I had to write," he was quoted as saying. "No one told me to. No one paid me to. And eventually someone took notice." Yes, they did:

- Leo Connellan won the Shelley Memorial Award from the Poetry Society of America.
- Leo was nominated for three Pulitzer Prizes.
- Leo was named the Poet-in-Residence for the CSU System.
- Leo was named the Poet Laureate of the state of Connecticut.
- And in his most recent triumph, Leo was named one of the one hundred most important writers in Maine's history.

Recognition came late in life for Leo Connellan. But when recognition came, it came profusely. Leo was proud that his work was recognized, but he was always a bit wary of the honors he received—and a bit worried that we in the CSU System would think he was no longer part of our team. Leo would call after 5 p.m.—when he knew I would be out of meetings—to tell me of his latest honor. It might be an invitation to lead a poetry workshop in New York. Or an invitation to read at the Sunken Garden Poetry Festival. Or to be given an honorary doctorate at a university in Maine. And he would begin, "You know, I'm on your team. I've got this invitation to be on Maine Public TV (and then go into a lengthy description.) But I just want to be part of your team. I hope you don't mind."

Mind?! Mind?! Of course not. Leo brought honor to the CSU System by being part of our team. He brought honor to the state by being its poet laureate.

But the honors Leo received, I think, were less important to Leo than the excitement and joy he felt when he was able to touch a young writer—to help young students understand poetry—and to understand that they, too, could write poetry. He would call—after 5—to share with me how he had been able to break through the skepticism of some students that they could ever understand—much less write—poetry. He would patiently explain to me—who has very little poetic sensibility—how he had patiently explained to his students what the words and images of a poem meant.

Probably the example I remember most involved his poem, "The Assassin." You know it. In its entirety, it reads:

I am hidden within
who you think I am.

And he would proudly tell me how he had asked the students what it meant, and how they eventually recognized that only someone who was thought to be part of everyday life would be allowed to come close enough to a victim to assassinate him.

We have files and files—probably dating back ten years and more—of letters from teachers and students telling us how much they enjoyed having Leo work with them. And providing confirmation that Leo had in fact helped them understand poetry, and had even persuaded them that they should try their hand at it. "Students see Leo as a real person working in the real world, able to focus his experiences so intensely and poignantly," one teacher wrote. Another said, "Leo doesn't write about roses and butterflies, but about life's struggles and relationships. . . . There's a hard edge. He's real, and his poetry's real. The students are moved." As one critic said in a review in the *Boston Globe*, Leo's poems "go straight to the heart."

One of Leo's closest friends reminded us that "No one brought poetry to more people than Leo. No pretense. Even though he was inwardly honored by being the Laureate, he never lost his style, his laughter and his wariness." Leo, his friend said, "hung around a long time, long enough to settle a few old scores and become the poet those in poetry power wouldn't allow him to become. He outwrote them and outpoeted them."

That he did. Leo Connellan is a state treasure.

Poetry Man

James Coleman

Leo was a big guy, broad-shouldered, carrying some fat when I first met him in the late seventies. He was in his fifties then, recently out of his long-time sales job, recently out of the drinking life. Leo was substitute teaching and sweeping the stairwells in his apartment complex to try to make ends meet, to support himself, his wife Nancy, and his daughter, Amy. Then, and until the end, Leo had an unusual presence, part of it born, certainly, of his many years of selling, part of it born of his familiarity with hard times. However, there was more to it. This essay will try to catch a few of the qualities that contributed to Leo's unusual command of audiences, his ability to strike through to people with his poetry, and person to person.

Tony, his landlord, had trouble believing that Leo was a famous poet. He didn't look the part, a point he often made to endear himself to an audience. Once he had trotted out the image of a "constipated water buffalo," the audience was completely enraptured. He was perhaps more bear-like, but that catches only a little of how it was to be with him. Like so many of the Irish, he could wear a pugnacious look. He might look aggrieved as he sat in a classroom chair, waiting to be introduced, yet he didn't look like a convincing thug. His hands were fine, the hands of a furrier or a jeweler or a poet, and they sent another message as he sat at the front of a class, distraught and overweight.

His father had been a postmaster, supervisor of other people's paper, and in Leo's poems, there is an urge to separate from the dutiful. He mocks the predilection of Irish-Americans to work in government jobs, as the way of living out the warped and authoritarian child raising promoted by the Catholic Church. Recent church scandals would not have surprised Leo, since he saw the church as spiritually maiming its congregants, cowing them, rendering them weak and servile. That some priests would transgress with children would only confirm Leo's larger analysis.

Leo was on the side of the oppressed, the pushed-around, and by implication the students who listened to him on his journeys to schools as poetry consultant to the Connecticut State University system. His remarkable success with young people from junior high to community college to the university was the product of something deeper than showmanship, and something more profound, perhaps, than poetry.

His mother died when he was seven. He was told that she had gone "to take care of a boy who needed her more than he did." When I think of Leo, I think of this story. Its poignancy and the inherent injustice of his father telling Leo that peculiar lie about his mother's death shaped Leo's view of the world, and the aesthetics of his poetry.

Besides that central story which he told and retold, my view of him is colored by the fact that he reminded me of my own father. He had the same Irish charm, the same salesman's manner. So he and I connected on several levels, probably in ways more complicated than I can fully sort out.

Irish and working class, Leo was an expressive and articulate person whose take on the world filled in the shadows and incompleteness of my own background. In 1917, at age fifteen, my father quit his work in a bakery in Pawtucket, Rhode Island, twelve hours a night, twelve cents an hour. He went to Maine to be a lumberjack, then quickly decided that was not his calling, and fled the woods. Back in Boston, he signed on with a truck convoy to the Midwest, and, once there, went to work in the fledgling auto industry. A generation later, Leo, the motherless Maine boy, left his home to cross America, to escape a life similar to the one my father had fled.

When I first received a poem from Leo, as a submission for *The Red Fox Review*, I recognized that a part of what I had been searching for in myself was expressed in Leo's work. Leo was a literary tough guy who'd fought his way up without degrees or posh schooling. In the cold universe of America, the "air-conditioned nightmare," and the strange world of American letters, Leo and I recognized that we had common origins and a common cause, and we tried to provide one another with support.

"Jimmy," he would begin, either when he called, or when we ran into each other, which we often did, at the supermarket, or when Leo would drop by the college. Then he'd tell me about some perfidy of the literary establishment, or we'd talk about our kids. He'd met my oldest through substitute teaching at the junior high, and his interest in young Jim was one of the serious bonds between us, one that never waned. Much later, Leo's advice helped to shape Jim's attitude toward his tough first year of graduate school. "Don't let anyone push you out, and when you get done, you'll be able to call your shots" was the essence of Leo's counsel. While Leo suffered mightily in his own life over slights and enmities, he had a genuine interest in our family, and was gruff and thoughtful in his advice-giving. But then we had the advantage and the privilege of living near Leo, and of having him as an occasional guest for coffee or lunch, when his labors in the world, or the world of poetry, were somewhat at bay.

Leo was proud that he had eluded the "nets" (as James Joyce called them) of his birthplace and community. In "Amelia, Mrs. Brooks of My Old Childhood," Leo is contacted by a friend of Mrs. Brooks (Amelia), who "admonishes" him for neglect of the woman who cared for him after his mother's death. "This one resents! She/ can't put her finger on it, but there's/ something in the loose free easy/ way I materialize at her door from/ miles away...." (*New and Collected Poems, 45*—hereafter *NCP*). He had gotten away from her type of woman, and she disliked it, Leo used to comment on these lines. His ability to open the door to freedom certainly influenced readers and listeners, even magnetized them.

In "In Lobster Night," the young poet, "just off train," is back in Maine for a visit, and he's taken in hand by Otto Fishinfolk who "can smell your fear of his violence/ if you don't come and makes you go/ with him stalking a night of lust" (*NCP 15*). Leo goes on, "He needs you violated, your/ life happiness spoiled" (*NCP 15*). This kind of camaraderie is something to "get away from," and yet the situation is complex:

You come home drawn back by
Need to come from some place
Even after you got away (*NCP 15*).

The Maine high school students who had a "Leo Club" may have heard a sibilant note in Leo's recitation of one or another of these poems, or others which treat the theme. He was physical about his reading. Often, he kept the meter with his index finger, and often he scowled at audiences as if daring them to risk missing the sense of the poem. He guided audiences through a range of responses, and they always seemed grateful, and even ennobled by being able to participate.

Leo's reading of "Old Gravestones," for instance, was a journey to understanding, from the bald incident of vandals kicking down cemetery headstones, to Leo's evocation of why "in raging anger our young kick them down... in rage against quick dismissal by us into/ earth forever with an old gravestone all that's/ left of them" (*NCP 188*). As we again court the death of the young in a distant war, Leo's unfolding of this poem has come to mind.

The above only sketches a few elements of Leo's brilliance with an audience, and the universal theme of escape into freedom his poems engage and clarify. One of his great comic performances is the poem "Motel" from his 1995 book *Provincetown* which uses the self-deprecating humor already mentioned to explore the strange attainment of freedom that Leo felt in later years, with steady work, and unexpected recognition. Here is an excerpt from Section II:

Here I was in a luxurious room with room service
and a balcony, but the maids in the hall when
I passed them saw penury in the set of my mouth fixed

forever in fatigue and endurance's look and
on their hands and knees scrubbing carpets
and the halls of the motel hallways, if they wanted

their jobs, one or two of these lovely ladies smiled
at me enjoying that one of them had somehow managed
to be a guest....(11-12)

Leo's iridescent spirit brightened the world immeasurably. He insisted that, as everyone could see, he was an ordinary guy who had made it through hard work. He sowed hope, respect for poetry and poets, and a deep awareness of the challenges of being human. To not work with him again is a sorrow, to have worked with him in the classroom a joy. And we still have the poems.

Perhaps the Irish in America will discover him, and claim him as the voice of their struggles that he surely is. He spoke truly for my salesman father, and for the people who want to believe that America is not, as F. Scott Fitzgerald put it, "essentially a cheat." Leo fought for all of us daily; he knew that hope and freedom were at stake.

Minor Notes:

1. Some of the time, being from Detroit, I was Leo's consultant on cars. Leo drove with the abandon of an old time road salesman to colleges and high schools to read his poems. He didn't have a company car, and he tended to drive cars to the last inch of their lives. A black Chevette he owned still sits outside an abandoned gas station on route 169. It was the car that shot its sparkplugs at the hood one by one as Leo tried to get it to take him to an evening reading. One of his cars veered strangely. One of them leaked all its gasoline on the Griswold High School parking lot, and caused the school to be evacuated. Another blared its horn at Central Connecticut State University all the time Leo was inside working. He came over one Sunday with a car running erratically, and his plans for Monday involved driving it a few hundred miles. I took off the air cleaner, saw nothing, and replaced it. Then the car wouldn't run. Leo pointed out that the car had run until I had gotten under the hood, which was true. I only had to rebuild the carburetor which had fallen apart when the air cleaner was removed. He used the cars like tanks in his battle with those who would take away what we deserve: rich, intelligent informed lives with love and justice in them.

2. I kept the manuscript of the still unpublished *Knapsack and Stars* at my house after the heat was turned off on Leo, Amy, and Nancy at the Riverview Apartments in Norwich while they sought shelter elsewhere.

3. Leo worried that writers pull their punches when they are fearful of offending someone. He cautioned his students and fellow writers about this.

4. I was always glad to hear Leo's voice or to see him crossing the lawn at Mohegan before a reading. I felt that Leo registered much of the world's perfidy and sorrow, which most of us can block more readily than he could. The early mother-loss may have left him without a tough skin.

5. He was large, he lived large, he wrote large. I hope his work will last. It deserves to, and it was hard-won by a man who gave himself to the work, and to the well-being of his family and friends, and to all those who took time to listen.

Leo Connellan and the Art of Self-Invention

Amy Connellan

Throughout my life, I have read many articles about my father, Leo Connellan, both about his work and about his life. However, none of the writers of these articles ever dealt with the one facet of Leo that I think is most important. In order to understand his personality, and to put his work into the context of his life, it is essential to understand that Leo tended to fictionalize his personal history. This may seem surprising, considering one of his greatest gifts was his ability to write unflinchingly about difficult topics. He detailed subjects like rape, child abuse, domestic violence, alcoholism and more with brutal honesty. Unfortunately, this unflinching honesty wasn't often applied when it came to relating his personal history.

I remember as a child being confused by the stories that Leo told his friends. I was aware that the things he said were largely untrue, but I could not understand why he was telling these untruths. As I grew older, I learned that most adults tell lies from time to time. I also grew to realize that most adults don't tell as many lies as Leo did, as frequently as Leo did. Sometimes Leo told stories in order to gain sympathy or to meet a desired end, but just as often he seemed to tell stories for sheer entertainment value. As an adult I can look at Leo's background, at his childhood, and comprehend what caused this need to fictionalize his life, and I can also appreciate how integral this knowledge is to understanding Leo's work.

In many ways, his work was driven by the demons of his childhood, by the death of his mother, and by the brutality of his father. But these same demons that compelled him to light the shadowed places of the human soul also caused him to spend his life racked with insecurity. He desperately sought reassurance and love, and he wasn't particular about what tales he told to get that reassurance and love. Unfortunately, many people believed these stories. Also, Leo told so many tales at so many different times that it's difficult to impossible to sort them out. Even Leo couldn't! He used to joke that my mother had better outlive him, because without her he couldn't remember which stories were true and which he'd made up. Like Hamlet, he would need her to "...tell (his) tale aright."

To Leo, the basic facts of one's life were merely statistical data, useful for identifying people, but of no use in determining who a person really "is." Growing up as the child of a dead mother and an abusive father, Leo learned to survive by figuring out what his father wanted. It is crucial to know this if one is to understand why Leo felt so free to alter the facts of his life to suit his whim. By telling half-truths and even outright lies, he could "keep the old man happy," as he was wont to describe it. Sometimes, these "factual revisions" were merely oversights. He often described his eleven "maiden" aunts in Maine, telling how their father ignored them, and how bleak their later lives were. Never mind that there were really only nine aunts (and not all of them were spinsters). The important thing was how they lived, and what their lives said about the lives of unmarried women in early twentieth century America. The factual truth was incidental to the greater human truth he was trying to expose.

Leo spent most of his life searching for human truth. He had a lifelong fascination with evil, constantly reading books about rapists, murderers and, especially, serial killers. But his was not merely a morbid curiosity, a desire to get a vicarious "thrill" by reading detailed accounts of torture and mutilation. Rather, he was seeking something deeper, the motivation for these acts. It has been postulated by some that such criminals are "created" by unspeakable childhood abuse. If this is true, then why do others who have suffered similar childhood trauma never commit violent crimes? How can a species capable of creating Mahatma Gandhi and Martin Luther King Jr. also create Adolph Hitler and Joseph Stalin? What is the essence of good? Of evil? These are the truths Leo was interested in, the basic truths of humanity.

Perhaps it is impossible to truly understand Leo without understanding the world that created him. Leo's father, James Connellan, was raised in Portland, Maine, the youngest child and only son of a well to do (and devoutly Catholic) Irish immigrant. He was a classically educated lawyer who fluently read Latin and Greek. Early in his life, he defied his father to marry a Protestant woman. After this woman later died in childbirth, he returned home to his father, certain that God had taken his wife to punish him for straying from the Church. He remained at home until he married Leo's mother in 1928.

Ida Carey was the tenth of twelve children born in Hallowell, Maine to another Irish Catholic immigrant. As an infant, she was sent to live in Rockland, Maine with her mother's sister and brother-in-law, who were unable to have children of their own. Although her aunt and uncle raised her, and treated her as a beloved daughter (Leo once told me that the first automobile in Rockland belonged to Ida, having been given to her by her uncle as a graduation present), they were never allowed to adopt her. When Ida married James, she was a thirty-five year old spinster schoolteacher.

According to family legend, James was actually engaged to Ida's younger sister, Christine, but suddenly broke off that engagement and married Ida instead. What is certain is that, when Leo arrived on November 30, 1928, his family tried to pass him off as a "five month" baby. In point of fact, Leo really was premature, weighing in at just over one pound at birth. But to believe that Leo (or any child) survived after just five months gestation (especially in 1928!) simply defies credulity. It is far more likely that Leo was born at seven months gestation (meaning that James must have impregnated Ida before they were married, which would certainly explain the sudden "bride swap"). James was terribly disappointed by his first-born son. A venal, spoiled man, he seemed to believe he "deserved" a big, strapping, healthy son, rather than the sickly, small one he'd gotten. Leo's aunt Christine later told him that Ida came close to leaving James because of the way he treated his infant son.

Fourteen months after Leo's inauspicious arrival, Ida delivered a second son, named James for her husband. The younger James was as hale and healthy as Leo was not, and quickly became their father's favorite. Ida was worn out from two difficult deliveries in less than two years, and died of double pneumonia in 1936, leaving her boys in the care of her husband. The boys were told that their mother had "gone away to take care of another little boy who needed her more" and not to "dare cry and upset that poor man" (their father). The loss of his mother and the inability to mourn her loss are really the defining events of Leo's life.

* * * * *

After a brief stint in the Army, Leo settled in New York City and spent the next several years traveling throughout the country, working a series of odd jobs and sleeping in shelters as he went. While he did write a few short stories during this time, the only real writing to come out of his travels was *Crossing America*, which he wrote in the 1970s. Most of the time traveling was spent in an alcoholic fog. It wasn't until he stopped drinking that he was able to begin writing.

Leo met and married my mother, Nancy Anderson, in 1961. Shortly after their marriage, they moved to California, living first with her father, and then in an apartment over the moving company warehouse that Leo managed. In 1964 they moved back to New York, settling into an apartment on Cornelia Street in Greenwich Village. Leo was newly sober, and my mother made a deal with him; she would go to work, and he would stay home, remain sober and try to write. She was hired as a caseworker for the City of New York Department of Welfare, where she worked until she became pregnant with me in 1966.

Probably as a consequence of losing his mother at an early age and being an object of derision for his father, Leo had a desperate need to be loved and approved of. In almost every situation of his life, he had a need to be seen in a favorable light. Any criticism was almost too much for him to take. He would deny vehemently having committed a small offense, such as putting an empty milk carton back into the refrigerator, behaving as though he were accused of something far more serious than a minor irritation. My mother and I would always gently tease him about these denials, apologizing with mock seriousness and insisting that Ping-Ping (one of our cats) must really have been the guilty party. Reassured by the teasing, his instinctive defense would crumble. "You've got to watch that Ping-Ping," he'd declare, his face alight with a devilish grin, "you can't tell what he'll get up to."

Another thing that needs to be known about Leo is that he was deeply religious. Although he stopped going to church sometime in the 1950s, Leo never truly left the faith of his childhood. Leo was an altar boy for nine years! Unfortunately, the Catholicism passed onto him by his father and by his "fire and brimstone" priest left Leo with a perpetually guilty conscience, even when he'd really done nothing wrong. In the late 1980s, Leo started to write *Knapsack and Stars*, his memoir of his years in New York and hitchhiking across America. At this same time, he began looking at me with a mournful (what he termed "hang-dog") face every time I entered his presence. When I would ask the reason for the look, he would merely sigh and say, "You know I love you, Chuck." (Because my middle name is Charlotte, Leo usually called me "Chuck" when we were in private.) I would agree that yes, I knew that he loved me, and he would reply, "Well, you wouldn't if you knew what I had done."

This routine continued for about a month, during which time I wracked my brain, desperately trying to think of what Leo could possibly have done that could (in his mind) make me stop loving him. Could he be hinting that he'd been in prison? Killed someone? Finally the great crime was revealed. With face downcast, he said, "I was married to someone else before I married your mother." He felt such guilt over his failed first marriage that he could not imagine that I would not hate him for it. If not for the fact that he was writing his memoir and planned to mention the marriage in it, I doubt he would ever have told me about this first marriage.

He desperately needed to be approved of, to be "right" in every situation. Once, when going through my old school records, Mother and I came upon a report by my nursery school teacher regarding a conference she'd had with Leo. In it the teacher wrote that my father "...tries to discipline Amy" but had great difficulty because my mother "...allows Amy to do whatever she wants." Mother and I still chuckle over that one. While my mother was hardly perfect, at least she understood that my love was not contingent upon getting what I wanted. It was Leo who could deny me nothing. As a child, Leo had to "buy" whatever little affection he got from his father, by doing or saying what his father wanted. Leo couldn't understand that I could and did love him simply because he was my father, and that I would always love him, no matter what. So, whenever Mother said "no," I always knew that Leo would wink, smile, and say, "Go ahead, Chuck. What your mother doesn't know won't hurt her."

Leo's desperate need for reassurance, coupled with his constant guilt, often led him to tell the most outrageous stories. He had an almost obsessive need to make people like him, and he would do or say almost anything to insure this would happen. During his forties, he (like many other men) had something of a "mid-life" crisis. Leo was no longer "young" (at least according to the standard of our society). Also, the dynamic of his marriage had changed with my arrival. I know Leo loved me, and was in awe of having helped create me, but he was also insecure and needed to be the center of attention in any relationship. With my arrival, my mother's attention was no longer focused solely on him. Also, for a man who worshipped the memory of his dead mother, my mother's new status as a mother created in Leo something of a Madonna complex.

For these and myriad other reasons, Leo began to seek the company of other women, and to tell these other women the typical "my wife doesn't understand me" tales. One of the funniest of these tales involved a woman in Rhinebeck, New York. Apparently, Leo told this woman that Mother demanded he provide her with "sirloin and strawberries." At the time, Leo was working as a traveling salesman while Mother stayed with me in our apartment in Brooklyn, New York. Leo was suffering frequent panic attacks, and was convinced that he was about to have a heart attack at any moment. Leo insisted that he needed to carry at least fifty dollars on him at all times, so that when the anticipated heart attack occurred the ambulance crew wouldn't think he was indigent. This meant that Mother was stuck at home all day with absolutely no money. She couldn't even afford a ten-cent cup of coffee when she'd take me for a walk in the park.

Leo told many tales like "Sirloin and strawberries" at many different times. However, it's imperative to note that Leo never told these tales with the intention of hurting my mother, or me, or anyone else for that matter. He told these tales because he was unable to believe that anyone could like or love him simply for who he was. Later in Leo's life, Mother and I would often tease him about some of the biggest "whoppers" he told. While Leo sat convulsing with laughter, Mother would cry (in mock indignation), "Sirloin and strawberries!? I was lucky to be eating cube steak!" As his laughter subsided, Leo would give Mother a sideways glance and say, grinning, "Here I am, your hero."

Leo Connellan was "... the best and the least of mankind" (*Shatterhouse*, VI). He was a gifted poet who painted the vast spectrum of humanity with a fierce compassion. He swept away convention and forced readers to see the underside of our society, and to feel the humanity of those who inhabit it. But Leo was also a human being, a "motherless child" raised in the black heart of the Great Depression by a father who had no affection for him. Leo despised falsehood and deception, yet he had absolutely no compunction about altering the details of his life for dramatic effect, because he'd learned as a child that survival meant telling people what they want to hear. He was a "... struggler and survivor" (*Shatterhouse*, VI) who conquered alcoholism twice and forged a career for himself in the cutthroat world of academe, despite having never graduated from college. But, most important to me, he was my father. And yes, Leo, you are our hero.

from *Negative Capability*, 1994

Living with Leo

Nancy A. Connellan

For many years Leo earned a living as a salesman. Before, after, and during these jobs he wrote poetry. But it was his persona as a salesman that made a notable impression on many people. I remember when one kindly intended minister's wife cautioned me not to expect too much from Leo's sales job. She said most salesmen were well-dressed, neatly coifed, and well organized; she then directed my gaze toward Lco who was seen striding down the street, hair awry, necktie blowing in the wind, a rumpled figure and one we all knew to be a stranger to organization.

Garrulous as well as gregarious, Leo enjoyed meeting strangers and he responded strongly to the challenge of a prospective sale. Surprising most of all the minister's wife, he was modestly successful as a salesman. Whether his sales were achieved through persuasion or by some form of attrition, we were not inclined to question when the God of Paychecks smiled upon us.

For others The Groves of Academe, The Ivory Tower, or even the romantic garret. For Leo and family, the "Groves" weren't open at that time. "The Tower" was inaccessible and even garrets had landlords.

As Leo metamorphosed into multiple sales selves, we always invented titles for him which were direct and definitive: Leo-Siding, Leo Ice Melt, Leo Lord Carbon-Papers, etc. The title that lingers in my mind is Leo Alarm. Leo worked briefly for a company which sold questionable alarm systems to people who questioned the intent of others. Happily severed from that employment a few steps ahead of the sheriff who closed the company doors, Leo went on to become Leo B. Chemical, Leo Check-Encoder, and eventually Leo-Phone-Speak (*not* a precursor to the Speaker-phone).

Many years have passed since Leo has had to make his living by sales, except for occasional Phone-speak (telemarketing) during economic dry spells, and all those salesmen with the given name, Leo, have faded from memory except for one: Leo Alarm. Now it is not the remembrance of those dreadful alarms that makes this title live on for me. No, it is Leo himself, an original human alarm system if there ever was one. It's not that he is interested in acting out a "Chicken Little" role. He knows the sky is not falling. He knows it as well as you do. It's just that he wants people to be aware of potential calamities and to glance up at the heavens every now and then.

Revision of an article in *Down East* magazine, November 1997

In The Clear Blue Lobster-Water Country with Leo Connellan

Christopher Corbett

Quite early on a gull grey morning the poet Leo Connellan, native son long in exile, meanders through Rockland, past the sites of his vanished youth. The Thorndike Hotel is gone now. Phil Sulide's pool hall and shoeshine stand is no more. Bill Sullivan's coal yard, too.

But down on the waterfront the gulls glide and dive and caw in the overcast morning, the fishermen, wearing rubber boots and aprons, smoke and swear and laugh over a story. Here Leo Connellan appears in a scene out of a Leo Connellan poem, a hardscrabble world of Maine's working poor that the tourists do not see.

Rockland is the old Penobscot Bay town that Connellan has immortalized. Hailed by *The New York Times* as "a voice for the working class," he may be the most original poet Maine has produced in this century, the most prominent since Edwin Arlington Robinson. Connellan, who turns 69 this month, is a genuine, native-born, voice for the voiceless. His poetry is filled with cannery workers and lobstermen risking their lives to eke out a living, young people forced to emigrate, a teen-age boy dead in a car accident, the dangerous life on a dragger or of drunks fighting at a country dance.

"Leo Connellan writes about a Maine that very few people write about," says William Carpenter of the College of the Atlantic in Bar Harbor. "He very much identifies with the working class. He's done a terrific job of honestly portraying the people of Maine."

As stony and immutable as the Rockland breakwater, Connellan is a big man, with a sad Irish face and a head covered with thinning grey hair. His soft pale, blue eyes peer intently through his wire-rimmed glasses.

“I made a decision to write about real people,” says Connellan, surveying the waterfront of his hometown. “When I was younger there was always an underclass in Maine that was never written about.”

Born in Portland, the grandson of an Irish immigrant who fled County Clare and the Potato Famine, Connellan came to Rockland as a child (his father was a lawyer and postmaster there). The two events that shaped Connellan’s life and poetry were the death of his mother when he was seven and growing up (albeit middle class) in then bleak, blue collar Rockland during the Depression. It was here that he learned to identify with the Maine that is not “the way life should be.” His is another vision of Maine, a bleak and hard vision but one laced with a deep love.

“He’s writing about the heroes of daily life, a woman working in a sardine cannery, as opposed to some college professor in his summer cottage writing about squirrels,” says Alexander Taylor, publisher of the Connecticut-based Curbstone Press, which published Connellan’s 14th book of verse, *Provincetown*, in 1995.

In the kingdom of American poetry that is dominated by academia, Connellan is a loner.

Leo Connellan is no academic poet. He’s gone his own way,” says Robert Farnsworth, a writer who teaches at Bates College in Lewiston. “Leo doesn’t play the circuit.”

Yet many major American poets, many academics, Karl Shapiro, Richard Wilbur and Phillip Levine, among others, have praised Connellan. He has read at Harvard and Yale and the New York Public Library. He has recorded his poetry for the Library of Congress.

Richard Eberhart, poet and longtime faculty member at Dartmouth College, once described Connellan this way: “Leo Connellan does not belong to the mainstream of university poetry for university-educated readers, but to another mainstream of American consciousness whose textbook is raw life and whose words can be understood by anyone.”

For years, Connellan would rise at 3 a.m. and write his poems. Day after day. And then spend the rest of the day in the Willy Loman world, working as a salesman for an office supply company, which went bust in the late 1970s, leaving Connellan in dire straits.

In the school of life, Connellan has done postdoctoral work, laboring variously as a dishwasher, janitor and trucker's helper. "I've lived on skid row and in missions. I've hoboed and panhandled," he says.

Today, by any standard, Connellan is a successful and important poet. Thrice nominated for the Pulitzer Prize, he was awarded the Shelley Memorial Award by the Poetry Society of America in 1983, a distinguished honor that places him in the rarefied company of Robert Penn Warren, Archibald MacLeish, Edgar Lee Masters and e.e. cummings. He was nominated by Connecticut's senior senator Christopher Dodd for the post of Poet Laureate of the United States this year (unbeknownst to Connellan). The Great American Publishing Society, based in Greenwich, Connecticut, is bringing out a CD collection of Connellan's work. A filmmaker has recently completed a film of Connellan's poem "Lobster Claw."

Although he has lived in self-imposed exile outside of Maine most of his adult life, Connellan is still Rockland's poet. On this quiet, cloudy morning, the distant islands of Penobscot Bay faint across the water, the sun a pale presence through the fog, he comes like a ghost to roam through the old town, tracing a little of his long ago life in this sea city.

Wandering along the waterfront, Connellan speaks passionately about his verse: "My poems are often about escape and loss . . . anger, outrage and heartbreak." He has been conducting a lover's quarrel with Maine for half a century. (There is no reconciliation in sight.)

The suggestion to Connellan that he tour the Knox County seat—the focus of his finest poetry—bluntly brings the response that the Rockland of his boyhood and his poems exists only in his head and on the printed page. But perhaps as much to humor an interviewer (he does not suffer interviewers gladly) Connellan agrees to a sentimental journey (he is the least sentimental of men). He was enroute from his home in Connecticut to Nova Scotia with his wife of 37 years, Nancy, to celebrate their wedding anniversary when he stopped in Rockland.

On Main Street in his hometown Connellan expects anonymity on this grey morning and so it astonishes him when a well spoken, older woman hails him like a long lost friend in front of The Second Read, a popular coffee bar/used bookstore that is part of a Rockland that you won't find in Connellan's poetry.

"I saw you read last year at the Farnsworth. You were wonderful," she says. Connellan is surprised and delighted to meet an admirer. The lady offers the observation that it does not matter what anyone in Maine or even Rockland thinks about Leo Connellan. "They didn't appreciate Louise Nevelson, either." she says of the famous artist, also a Rockland exile.

By mid-morning, Connellan seems to warm a bit to the idea of touring Rockland. At the post office there is a plaque commemorating his father's term as postmaster signed by Franklin Delano Roosevelt. Connellan lingers here and chats with the clerks about mutual acquaintances.

On Park Street, he is reminded of the past that haunts his verse. "This was where Amelia Brooks lived, right here," Connellan says. She is the Madonna of one of his most powerful poems—"Amelia, Mrs. Brooks of My Old Childhood."—a paean to the hard life of working on the coast of Maine. Perhaps no poem of Connellan's, perhaps no poem written about Maine people, more powerfully captures the brave dignity of the working poor.

> Great lady of Sardines and
> earth and blood of
> Blueberryin' years, Clam Factory
> years who brought up
> children without help, a hopeless
> husband beating you in
> his futility . . .
> Amelia, lady of poverty and no hope,

saint of this earth if ever there
is a saint and if not then you
are what was always instilled in us
as what a saint is, woman in the
retinas of God's eyes for your simple courage
and great accomplishment with no money . . . .

Connellan is plainly moved by the old neighborhood. He lived around the corner. His poem was based on a real person and like everything in his work, deeply rooted in his own life.

A tour of his old haunts takes him down to the South End which offers a spectacular view of the harbor and the clear blue lobster-water country beyond. Connellan stops before a great vacant house that looks like the Edward Hopper painting "Haunted House" which hangs in the Farnsworth Museum. It is a house blasted by abandonment and neglect, paint gone, windows vacant, the dooryard weed filled. This is the landscape of Connellan's Maine. Nearby is the facility used by Outward Bound. It is testament to Connellan's sense of Rockland (a world that for him stopped half a century ago) that he has never heard of Outward Bound.

Long a resident of Connecticut, Connellan now serves as poet-in-residence for the Connecticut State University System and as Connecticut's Poet Laureate. In Connecticut that's a real job, a position of authority and prestige. "He's done stunning things with secondary school students. He's turned kids on to poetry," says Taylor.

In Connecticut, Connellan has thrived. But in his native Maine, he notes wryly, he remains something of a prophet without honor. Robert Woodbury, then president of the University of Southern Maine, approached Connellan about a position which would have allowed him to return home in 1984 but it never worked out. And so, Connellan remains, what a critic writing here in *Down East* once called "Maine's greatest living unknown poet."

Later, sitting in The Second Read before a steaming mug of black coffee, Connellan is oblivious to Rockland's trendy transformation.

Wearing jeans and a dark blue T-shirt, he looks slightly out of place here and that may be what makes the average reader so comfortable with him and why his readings are so popular. "He really connects with a Maine audience. He's riveting," says Constance Hunting, editor/publisher of Puckerbrush Press in Orono.

Connellan's greatest gift as a poet, his gift to Maine, is that he brings to poetry a fresh and original voice, a voice that, angry as it may often be, deeply loves Maine. "Leo makes people believe that poetry still matters," says Robert Farnsworth. "And that it's not just an academic parlor game. He's completely and utterly authentic."

Connellan hits it off with just plain folks (he got a standing ovation in Orono last spring) because he looks (and sounds) like he could be working on the Rockland waterfront, (except most waterfront workers do not quote Dante, Francois Villon and William Butler Yeats).

"Lots of people are afraid of poetry, intimidated," says Taylor, publisher of Curbstone Press. "But people are turned on immediately when they encounter a poet like Leo Connellan. They're hungry for this kind of poetry."

Critics often comment on Connellan's powerful link with real people. "He is the poet of the American working class who is as sophisticated as any of the elite but who has retained working-class values . . ." the poet Hayden Carruth wrote in the prestigious literary review *Parnassus*.

Connellan's reluctance to draw attention to himself (a very Maine quality) may explain why he is not well known. Assured that his books are for sale in Rockland, he shakes his head and says that couldn't be. But a check of the Reading Corner on Main Street shows copies of *Provincetown* and *The Clear Blue Lobster-Water Country*—available. This last long poem has been hailed as his masterpiece. A laudatory full-page review in *The New York Times Book Review* (unheard of for a book of poetry) compared Connellan to Robert Lowell.

"Once you leave Maine, your heart can be there, but there's nothing for you.... But I still carry Maine inside of me, enough to write these poems," says Connellan. And so he has written just such a poem of exile:

> . . . Yet back across Kittery bridge,
> things to do still must be
> and I can't come home until they're done.

Connellan knows that he may never come home again but he also knows that he has given the people of Maine his heart. He quotes his old mentor, the poet Karl Shapiro: "A poem is an anonymous gift to an anonymous recipient and when you've finished with it it doesn't belong to you."

Leo's Terrific Growl

Robert Creeley

I dare now to write this note of respect and affection for my good friend and truly indomitable fellow poet, Leo Connellan, not because he's dead and needs it, but because I come, however faintly, from Maine too, and know the kind of faith he kept and the complex life he had in that conduct. Sadly, we got to know one another only toward the end of his life, and that only by telephone. I cannot now remember who started it, but at least for those last years, we often talked in the way one might at the bar or the local diner. He'd call and I'd answer, and he'd ask me if the missus minded him calling, and I'd say that she didn't. It was an old time ritual, almost as though we were giving the requisite password, before we then settled into a review, often critical, of all the poets we knew the names of and their various activity.

Be it said, I knew how he felt, although it feels pretentious even to say so. There can be a sentimental recognition almost, of someone who has worked hard for something, earned it, so to speak—and that has its righteous application. In like sense, there's the natural, the one who was just born lucky, who caught the ball, played the music, danced all night by mere gift of existence—and never seemed not to be able to do anything. But Leo was a poet both by ability and intent. He wanted to be a poet and he was. Talking to him, I always felt that was clear. His other life, so to speak, the grit and particular work he'd done, his hard times with alcohol, all the facts of his day to day living, I knew very little of at all.

These details, call them, are certainly an apparent part of his poems and are even thought to be its foundation. Yet Leo takes one to a place, not a record. His poems are where he locates his life, not where he thinks to write about it. In his long and uniquely accomplished poem, *The Clear Blue Lobster-Water Country: A Trilogy* (1985), the narrator, hearing that a woman who had, when he was a child, been good to him is in difficulty, manages to come back and to find her as she is about to die. He speaks to her, tells her of his remembering her, of what she'd meant to him. But he cannot forgive her for, as he feels, abandoning him, for not then saving him, the motherless child. So he goes away, unannealed, as it were—not looking back and not being able to stay.

I may well change the text in my own mind, recalling it now in memory. It was such an ice-clear moment as I read this, knowing, with neither explanation nor comment, what the relation was between the two, how the narrator felt it, then and still, in its literal place, in himself. I can't imagine how Leo himself felt, writing of the sad facts, how he'd been able to hold on to such impacted, painful details. The story is real in the poem as little else ever is, in any place at all—as palpable, as present, as my sitting here now, trying to make that power evident. As always one needs to go read the poem for oneself.

There were times and honors in Leo's life, which recognized him for who and what he was, and for what he had, against odds indeed, managed to get done. I wish I had had chance to know him where he lived, gone with him to the places he visited, either in his employment at Connecticut State University or as State Poet of Connecticut, or visiting friends, or just walking around the town. He came back to Maine toward the end of his life, and there is a wonderful Maine Public Television documentary, which shows him looking around Rockland where he grew up, talking with friend Sandy Phippen, and then reading his poems at a local hall. He looks solid, a bit wary, answers questions with reflective, wry caution, seems familiar and at home. Over the years Maine has included its impressive artists and writers as Leo, as Marsden Hartley, for example, although what finally to do with them has been another question.

Talking about other poets, I remember particularly Leo's care for Richard Wilbur and Hayden Carruth. He felt both were honest and they in turn had recognized and respected him. Expectably he did not like or find company with any poetry 'school' and gave me the great credit of being other than my identity card might argue. He was a loner and saw others most clearly in the same condition. Tom McGrath was and is a measure of what Leo felt was the point and argument for any of it.

Otherwise he is presumed to be a 'simple' poet. Yet his resources, and that which he has to say, are hardly ever so. Whether in his stories or their means of telling or the language itself, there's a depth of effect and feeling, which does not come from a generalizing reduction. One quick example can be found in a short poem, "Scott Huff," which ends:

> ...God, if you need him
> take him asking me to believe in
> you because there are yellow buttercups,
> salmon for my heart in the rivers,
> fresh springs of ice cold water running away.
> You can have all these back for Scott Huff.

That's not at all simple to do. Take the weave of the "im/in" rhyming, the short "i" so flattened, the backbeat of the rhythm, the way things resist almost physically 'completing"—until the last line with its threes ("You can have/all these back/for Scott Huff") ends it all, thought, feeling, song. Or rhyming "Scott Huff" and "buttercups." It's as though he were swimming in the words, moving physically in their accumulating 'river.'

It's a good way to go, poetry—singing, even in Leo's terrific growl. Perhaps you'll come visit downeast some time? Please remember to bring some books of his with you. He'd like that and so would I.

LEO CONNELLAN: A LION'S COMPASSION

G. Scott Deshefy

In trying to sculpt my Renaissance life from an age of specialization, two close friends and mentors helped me illuminate those sometimes divergent byways: the late ethologist, Allen W. Stokes, and former Connecticut poet laureate, Leo Connellan. I first met Leo in 1996 outside a small bookstore in eastern Connecticut during one of his book signings for *Provincetown*. His expression metered somewhere between Irish insuperability and stoicism at the time. The event, not well publicized, had drifted into a thick and prolonged lull, the kind of foggy suspended animation that glazes the eyes. But for the two of us and ephemeral staff of a few businesses, the mall was a sea-becalmed. Leo, irrepressible as ever, continued to hold court. Arms folded defiantly, he sat motionless beside an unadorned folding table, the lone wolf poet wearing robes of a martyr.

In 1996, I had been hosting a biweekly poetry series at a coffeehouse in downtown Norwich called the Liberty Tree. For a month or so, I had toyed with the idea of inviting the newly appointed Connecticut poet laureate to read. Given the smallness of the venue, however, and its lack of honoraria, I doubted that Leo would accept. Nevertheless, seizing the opportunity, I bought a pair of coffees and pulled up a chair. For the next two hours, we discussed verse from Francois Villon to Emily Dickinson to Ferderico Garcia Lorca; and in the space of that time, Leo lectured me on the value of allusion, his lifetime of sacrifice for his art, the perpetual example of linguistic sleight of hand in his small poem, "Assassin." We became fast friends that day and allies in the exhibition of our work ("you watch my back and I'll watch yours," he would say). And I admired him for the hard road he had traveled to late recognition, the odd jobs he had performed to write in spare moments, the slightly tragic role of the outsider he played as if it were King Lear. Leo Connellan savored his post of esteemed "literarian" as only a Cubs fan could appreciate a championship so long overdue. Yet, in addition to the integrity of his work, he was immensely generous and accessible as poet laureate. He would often see the sun rise, get behind the wheel of an old car and drive the length of the state to teach poetry to youngsters. And yes, that grassroots poet of the common man, that master purveyor of the backstreet lingo of American sufferance, would graciously give one of his best readings en route to selling a score of books at the Liberty Tree...with one caveat, of course. If anyone asked, he "got his usual fee."

Leo Connellan could be cantankerous at times, a sage curmudgeon like H.L. Mencken generously peppered with the blunt skepticism of a David Hume. His blue-collar emergence as one of America's esteemed voices came late, after many years of pre-dawn writing, sometimes before selling vacuum cleaners or typewriter ribbons door-to-door. In discussing Leo Connellan's work, many will speak of his Holy Grail quest for a father's approval (so vividly displayed in *Clear Blue Lobster-Water Country*) or the sometimes estranged, ever-delinquent recognition by his academic peers. I choose instead a different tack for this essay. The facets I most admired in Leo Connellan's character, still tutoring us in his work, were his unwavering trust in his readers, his honesty as a writer and his tremendous compassion for the downtrodden (both human and nonhuman). He was, in my estimation, the kind of poet whom Harold Bloom would call a "strong poet," a man, who despite his hard knocks, was a Utopian at heart, a man, who could neither tolerate nor reconcile through metaphysics a world filled with victims and suffering, a man whose sensitivity, born from his own artistic and familial struggles, was all-encompassing. Let us briefly examine that part of Leo Connellan's work which his wife, Nancy, daughter, Amy, and closest friends knew so well, a compassion not only for human beings, but, more tellingly, for nonhuman animals, as well.

I begin with a theme (dichotomy really) which Leo explores in many of his poems, the dehumanizing effects of the commerce of killing. The poor and unlucky for whom Leo writes are both the fish and the fishermen. Clearly, the fish and crustacea suffer most, cruelly torn from their seas and garroted by air. But the fishermen, the carriers of that disease of brutality, become afflicted with a dark parasitism that consumes their humanity. Part of their tragedy is a loss of freedom to advance their culture through themselves. He who baits the traps casts, then the hooks and nets in search of commerce, kills because he knows no other life. He has never sought another training. Trapped by that lack of education, the fisherman's survival hinges on a morally depleting lifetime of destruction. He is no longer a human being, but reduced to an instrument of large-scale suffering in the hopes of minimizing his own. The fisherman is indentured to an economy of exploitation, unwilling or unable to escape the Maine which Leo himself had abandoned in youth.

We learn in Connellan's poetry that fishermen are both to be pitied and to be loathed. They are exploiters of nature, dispassionate in a hard and dangerous life, outcasts of humanity doomed to obsolescence by the very technologies of which they are part. Now, the very populations they plunder have fallen below sustainability, a "technology takin' too much" to use Leo's phrasing in the poem, "Lobster Fisherman." The American dream of a decent livelihood has become twisted into a nightmare of subsistence through slaughter, inescapable and deplorable. In "Lobster Claw," Leo writes:

> Lobster, I will kill you now,
> crouch in your rocks. Pull up
> your bed covers of seaweed.
> Ride the sea's bottom. Move
> out deep in winter. Burrow
> in mud. Hide under
> kelp. I will bait you
> to my family's survival
> without conscience. My own
> life is in the lines hauling you in...

Then, in "Provincetown," Leo asks us to look into the mirror of our own anthropocentrism. How can the takers of so many billions of nonhuman lives be appalled by a little *quid pro quo*, even when the exchange rate, the currency of human life, is disproportionately high? Why the horror? In "Provincetown," Leo cleverly affronts our species' monumental avarice. When the fishing community is dismayed by fate and nature making the slightest attempts to adjust an inequity, their reaction of surprise seems audaciously ludicrous and irrational. I like Leo's subtle, perhaps unintended, hint at animal rights:

...They come up on a wreck
and when the net caught they didn't
get fast enough to the winch
so rolled over and
stripped of their flesh by fish

The leg bone of Fisher Motel Man's father
come up in a net of fish catch
brought to Provincetown and identified
by X-ray records as Fisher Motel Man's father
...and the horror of holding

Your own father's leg bone picked clean
by the fish you hunt, as you pick
a chicken leg, pork chop, barbecue spare ribs clean
but they're supposed to be things to eat, always
human reckoning is ability to fathom fair is fair but

necessity, these people earn the food their children
eat fishing and scream in horror that God might
want dumb fish to have one of us every few ton...

This is the beautiful craftsmanship of Leo Connellan's work. In a cloak of irony, a philosophy of compassion (almost neo-Pythagorean or Jain-Buddhist) is entrusted to his reader. It is a compassion with which he does not bludgeon, but waits patiently for the reader's embrace. Final conclusions are not divulged necessarily, but open to syntheses via literary prompts. In "Lobster Claw," the fisherman admits to having no conscience because Leo trusts his readers to fill that void with their own. Ultimately, at the conclusion of the same poem, even the fisherman must arrive at his own guilt: "...Lobster,/ scavenger crustacean,/ why should I so mind/ killing you!"

In "Fish," that tinge of ethics, subjugated by the need to make a buck, resurfaces again in an admission of unholy commerce. The destroyers of fish are themselves destroyed by their own despair. A lifetime of administering death is dehumanizing, bleak and decadent. "We are the dead after the dead," the fisherman must concede.

There are many other examples of Leo Connellan's compassion for nonhuman animals juxtaposed with our own species' plight. In "Squirrel Shoot," Leo denounces the social evil of hunting (using capital letters to denote his pantheon of victims):

> High in the trees, the Squirrels would suddenly
> jolt in their tree to tree springing, as our guns
> crashed against the fragile ribs of their life, dropping
> them to our feet of exultation, like great laughter gone limp.
> Until we were, then, no longer boys, come to know that
> Squirrels should live and Deer and Fish and you and me.

In "Dark Horses Rushing," he draws similar parallels, this time using Mathew Brady's stills from the American Civil War: "...and the blue-coat boy shot him dead/ standing up like a despicable fox hunter...."

That "Squirrel Shoot" is a page away from "Shooter" and "Home Again" in Leo Connellan's book, Provincetown, may be no accident. Are the connections among the legalized violence of hunting and the legalized violence of war in "Dark Horses Rushing" and "To War Dead" assigned a deliberate proximity to the "unpermitted" slaughter of our own kind?

In "Shooter," Leo writes:

> Sometimes we hit and sometimes we get hit. A
> bullet just rolled off my roof. You go to
> Columbia University, I go to the undertaker.

And in "Home Again"

> ...He wanted
> to see what was left of where his
> Grandfather settled, now stripped shells,
> hollow buildings with too many holes in them
> for echoes. The skulls were out in their skin heads
> and four or five walked around his car, pulled
> machine pistols and made sure he stayed
> in the neighborhood.

In "Lament for Federico Garcia Lorca," dedicated to a poet whose work and courage Leo deeply admired, the cruelty of the great Spaniard's death is described in terms of tortured cats and butterflies smashed against walls.

That is not to say that expressions of compassion in Leo Connellan's poems are motivated by or predicated on "carry-over" violence against our own species in the form of drive-by shootings or Fascist executions. The fabric of that compassion is unstained by self-preservation. For starters, we need only look to the condemned bird in "A Hen Crossing a Road" or the enslavement of frogs in "The Frog Jump at Lisbon Central School". More conspicuously, there are the dockside bars, the seacoasts of Leo's boyhood Maine, drawing the full thunderous powers of his empathy. Great copper rods are in the seascapes and the waves there, the suffering of fish and lobster, marine mammals and fowl.

In "In Lobster Night," Leo paints death in the vulgarized colors normally associated with life:

> We drove into green woods. The lobster
> were shedding their claws. Little mosquitoes
> hovered over our sweat and had us like
> over ripe fruit. In the woods, in dead
> green, the dull dark green Maine winter
> does to green, and murdered lobster
> thrashing their lives out in the traps
> of the bay does to green, taking the
> bright life from the land that
> allows death in the sea.

Again, in "Lobster Claw," the harshness of the sea is a maternal defense of the innocent from the onslaught of fishermen:

> It is the sea mother
> who whips him in a
> wrath of wind like a
> snarling cat
> while lobstermen
> rip out her children.

From shelled and clawed we go to finned and scaled. In "Penobscot

Raccoons," Connellan describes the feverish pace of high-volume, assembly line killings, the mutilation business of Sardine factories, workers "like raccoons scurrying" in bleak, desperate conditions:

...women sitting across the conveyer
belt slice off herring heads and tails
and are paid for the speed they
can load up racks of the flake trays.
The fish do not know it, their
life strangled from them forced
into oxygen. What we live on kills
another as our head under water
of their world kills us...

Again, the carnage of herring is reiterated, taking its human toll, as well, in "Amelia, Mrs. Brooks of My Old Childhood." The woman, whose beauty Connellan so admired in his youth, is slowly immolated by the physical and unsavory work of the sardine factory, a stressful tedium. Leo suggests that the decomposition is moral and ontological as well as ontogenetic:

We sneak death again,
kill...take
herring from the sea our
boat circling, the Cannery
boats lifting the sardines
aboard onto their holds
through hoses...

Amelia, the fish have less
chance than you had
except your death would
be more subtle, you died
from it, Amelia, died from exhausting
survival, your life wearing
out your life...

Sitting in draughty cold
snipping off dead fish heads and tails
with scissors...

Amelia, how could you love
Maine, the blood blue ocean,
the black green pines and
fresh yellow and green
dandelions with your nose
plowed in the earth or
in the stink of the
dead of the sea.
Although you were no whore
You were as exploited
And paid for piece work...

In "Provincetown," Leo draws momentary attention to another cerebral species, the "collateral damage" of dolphins ("mammals like us") slowly drowning in tuna nets, inadvertent but avoidable casualties of commercial fishing were it not for the massive scale of that eco-larceny, the wanton, high-tech destruction of ecosystems by modern trawlers, canneries afloat. Center stage in "Provincetown," however, and a special place in many of Connellan's poems belongs to his fraternity of gulls. In "Provincetown," as if visited by Poe's raven, a broken-winged gull appears to the Connellans at their motel, haunting them with its mortal injuries. Moreover, no one, including the Audubon Society, will take reasonable efforts to try to save the bird's life. Unlike Motel Woman and other guests at the motel, who have hidden the bird's plight behind walls of denial and closed curtains, Leo cannot shut his eyes to the grief:

...Motel Woman who must have known
she risked our not only checking out immediately
but railing against her place to everyone else stood

Fast in her shrug, so, a big lovely sea gull
can't fly, has caught death, she pushed the horror
of it out of her head...

...We were told coldly by
Motel Woman we could feed it if we wanted to,
like, pushing it from herself, how could

we sit and breathe in and enjoy with a
creature of God's dying standing almost silent
weak and not vanishing but Motel Woman,
not wishing to lose customers, put it on us....

That at least we could feed it until it
finally gasped and rattled and fell over.

In "A Witness," Leo finds himself similarly distressed, drawing parallels to human struggle through avian embodiment:

Sea Gulls beating wings
I saw you dying...
Flew into a wall you did not understand
that springs on all of us
who might have won
alone and unsurrounded, fighting,
if we knew what was to be beaten.

But, in "Sea Gulls Wait," Leo puts death aside. His fascination with the gulls becomes a spiritual awakening to their resilience. A mutualism builds between author and birds in "Sea Gulls Wait." To Leo the birds are omnipotent, Sea Gull-gods calling him back to the Maines of his youth, companions in an inebriate's desert somewhere in Arizona, seen and heard in drunk tanks, wheels of freights, everywhere that humans struggle without reprieve by wealth or privilege. I read this poem and feel the coalescence of Leo's compassion for nonhuman animals merging with his own pains, a synthesis of the human ordeal. Maine has become a dark sun about which he must orbit like a bleak planet, held to that sun by faint gravities of hope, the desires to have known better his mother and father. Disappointed with each perigee that brings him closer to his boyhood memories, he is a scavenger of his own past, a gull both buffeted and buoyed by the coastal sea air, the anguish of failure under every success.

In a back cover quote, Leo Connellan once described my work as putting a "finger on old information." A big part of our friendship may have been my familiarity with facts and personalities more akin to Leo's generation than my own (the product, perhaps, of a three-generation household). When Leo wrote of actor Brian Donlevy's Heliotrope Harry ("Old Orchard Beach Maine Burned Down") or Don Bragg (an old pole vaulter like myself) in "Before Fiberglass," I could relate. Whenever we talked about Mickey Mantle ("The Whole Thing About Jedge's House") or the shoddy difference between modern ballplayers and the warrior-icons of the Fifties, we found common ground. I miss those conversations with Leo. History was important to him, a golden thread in his poetry. To employ allusion, as Leo would preach, it helps to be an aficionado of the past. We often discussed how modern, abridged versions of history can be a danger to current poetry, particularly in the myopic, pictorial society we bemoan.

In *The Clear Blue Lobster-Water Country* (Book II, "Shatterhouse," VI), Leo Connellan uses Stephen Crane to recall John Donne's "no man is an island," connecting the dots of our responsibilities as men and women. To whomever or wherever suffering occurs, we are conjugate. We cannot close a curtain to our responsibilities as the Motel Woman tried to dismiss the existence of a dying gull. Where suffering occurs, we must try to alleviate it. When we are haunted by our personal ghosts, we must confront them, as well. These are the philosophies of Leo Connellan's work, his greatest legacy. As with the early Greeks, he does not try to rationalize downtrodden lives by blaming the victims. Tragedy in Leo Connellan's poetry is not an unavoidable consequence of existence (as Schopenhauer might have argued). Our lives may be compromised by contending historical forces at times, as with the fish and the fisherman, but there is no metaphysical force of destiny at work. Tragedy, at least, can be minimized. The only obstacle is that we may not always be free to choose our course of action easily, and therein lies Leo Connellan's anger, the snarling of a great poet, a "strong poet," a lion in the desert roaring against the impending sandstorm. I read Leo Connellan's poetry and think of Nietzche towards the end of his life, an existentialist defender of the masses hugging an abused horse in the streets of Turin. It is a poetry opposed to killing of any kind, a milestone for survival, a primer for honesty and compassion writ large.

LEO REMEMBERED

Franz Douskey

It's right to write this, near Christmas Eve, at the edge of winter. I think of Leo a lot in the winter. Leo and his cars, rejects from Rent-A-Wreck, old relics that had to be coaxed to start in the gray mornings so Leo could go to the various schools throughout Connecticut and breathe life into poetry and into the students. Cars that knew the way home. In some ways, Leo was a relic, a reject from Rent-A-Wreck. Leo was never pretty. A hulking, awesome being lurching back and forth down the corridors of middle schools and high schools. But when Leo sat down with students, he took on the presence of a great teacher, a gentle human who had all the experience and the knowledge of words to pass onto younger writers.

Leo and I knew each other for thirty years, as well as any two outsider, Roamin' Catholic poets can know each other. He was a man who battled all the time. This planet was not an easy place for Leo. There were the poets who would not help, and others who could not help. But throughout his life Leo was blessed with great people. William Packard, the editor of *The New York Quarterly*, was an early friend to Leo. Bill published Leo in practically every issue of the *Quarterly*. John Baringer issued Leo's *Penobscot Poems* in 1974, which was a major stepping off point for Leo's successful run as a published writer. And Vivian Shipley was a constant, important supporter. There was Paul Zimmer who, as Editor of the University of Pittsburgh Press, published Leo's first major collection.

In the last decade of Leo Connellan's life, two friends stepped up and made Leo's poetry career significant and enduring. Andy Thibault arranged to have Leo edit a weekly poetry column in the T*orrington Register-Citizen*, and Andy was a significant force in Leo being named Connecticut's Poet Laureate. Another major ally, who often worked behind the scenes, was William Cibes, Chancellor of the Connecticut State University System. With Andy and Bill looking after Leo, he no longer had to struggle to stay afloat, at least financially.

There are a few pictures of Leo and me together taken over the years. You will note that neither one of us is looking at the camera and that we are both laughing. Leo was one of the funniest people I knew. We would go off into a corner somewhere and talk. He was not funny in a stand-up comic way. It was his vision of the planet, his insight into the way people played out their lives that was funny. Once Leo and I were asked to read at the Governor's mansion. A secretary called and told Leo what time he was expected to read. Then she added, as a way of admonishing Leo in case he might read one of his poems about real people, 'Mrs. O'Neil has requested 'no sex'." To which Leo responded, "Don't worry. I hardly know the woman."

Leo was complex, and even his darkness was pleasurable. His poems were most often about beaten people, awkward, struggling, who, at one time perhaps were capable of love. And because of his poems, some people, intentionally kept at a distance by Leo, thought that was what Leo was like. But he called himself "El Bardo," master of the Rimlets, a heretofore unknown poetry form, scathing, economical gems designed to prick up the ears of his literary dissenters: "Roses are red, violets are blue, how much better would the world be without you?" There are others containing specific names. Perhaps a courageous editor will publish Leo's *rimlets* someday, lawsuits and reputations be damned.

Leo had some fears, the worst of which were reviews with misquotes, substitution of ideas and actualities. He feared the terrible vindictiveness of failed writers who had become literary critics. But toward the end of the 20th century, Leo didn't let anything trip him up. He was writing better than ever. People wanted to publish his books and he was teaching students the magic and value of words. Except for another old car that had to be coaxed to start in the gray hoarfrost of New England weather, Leo began to take pleasure in each day. He lost weight. Had given up drink for years. He loved being feted. At a reception at a socialite-wannabe's mansion, Leo looked around at the huge rooms, the ceiling to floor velvet-draped windows, the people milling around and said to me, "Duke, we're rounding third and we're heading for home."

Winter nights seem quiet now. The phone doesn't ring. Sometimes it was hard to love Leo, but it was always harder not to.

The Ache of Exile

Christopher Fahy

One day in the early 1970s, a few years after I'd moved to coastal Maine, I was checking some books out of the Rockland library—possibly poetry books, I don't remember—when the librarian told me she'd gone through grammar and high school with someone named Leo Connellan who was now a poet. The library had some of his books, she said, and she thought they might interest me. So back to the shelves I went and found them and took them home.

I still remember the jolt I felt, like a splash of cold ocean spray in my face, when I opened the first of those books. Here was the Maine of rugged individualists, of decent, hard-working people, yes, but also the Maine I hadn't read about before: a mean, dark Maine of scrawny "farmwives and fishwives," of lobstermen who wouldn't hesitate to take a shot at those who messed with their traps. Here were the boozers and brawlers and fornicators—Leo himself included. People like these, who were sometimes part of the backdrop in sophisticated, genteel writing about Maine, were front and center in Leo's work.

There was nothing sophisticated about these poems, nothing abstruse or incomprehensible. Their lines were filled with raw power and brutal truth—as well as amazing tenderness—and I found them highly disturbing. No matter how strong we are and how hard we fight, they seemed to be saying, in the end it all comes to nothing. So much of his work dealt with loss, disappointment, failure and broken dreams.

As I read more of Leo, especially the narrative poems in *Death in Lobster Land* and *The Clear Blue Lobster-Water Country*, I learned of the primal loss that informed his work: the death of his mother when he was seven years old. Leo's father, unable to bear the terrible truth and hoping, perhaps, to spare his son the pain that he himself was feeling, told Leo his mother had gone away to care for another boy who needed him more than Leo did. So: loss, abandonment, betrayal, death—all woven deeply into Leo's work.

In 1977, Leo and I had poems appear in the same anthology. One day, out of the blue, I got a phone call. 'When I read that poem I said to myself, 'Who is this Christopher Fay-hee?"' the voice said suspiciously. My poems in that collection were both about Maine, and I sensed that I'd crossed a line I shouldn't have—was trespassing on Leo's turf. But Leo told me he'd soon be reading in Rockland and would like to meet me.

The reading took place at the Farnsworth Art Museum—and it was dynamite. Afterwards we talked for a while—not long—but Leo said he would keep in touch.

Now Leo's "keeping in touch" was legendary, especially back then, when he was, in his words, "a salesman for Schenley." He'd make call after call to friends and poets and critics and editors daily. He'd hound reviewers relentlessly until they finally cracked and wrote about his work. He'd think nothing of calling people at two in the morning. He didn't do this to me, and didn't call often, but when he did, I usually found what he said perplexing, dismaying—or boring. His predominant theme was himself and his work; it was almost as if nobody else existed, as if he were the world, perhaps the entire universe. "A lot of poets are faggots," he said to me once, "but I'm not," and then he proceeded to list those who were. "If you don't like me, I understand," he said. "Who wants to be friends with a paranoid schizophrenic?"

Leo wasn't schizophrenic, but paranoid? Maybe too strong a word, but let's put it this way: he never quite trusted people, never could quite believe that they liked his work—or him. "I'm doing what all these other poets wanted to do," he said to me, "and they hate me for it."

Maybe his deeply suspicious nature was born in his father's terrible lie about his mother, that primal betrayal, I really don't know. All that I know is, sometimes Leo saw me as a friend and sometimes he didn't. Why he did or didn't was a mystery. One time, when I thought we were getting along just fine, he wrote, "What have I done wrong? Tell me!" I had no idea what had sparked this question, and conveyed my confusion to him. A long stretch of silence then, but the next time I saw him, no friction at all between us. Then the following time, years later, years with no calls or correspondence, he was utterly cold, glaring at me with his squinty eyes and sour mouth. A few years after this he called and talked to me as if I were his long lost best pal.

An urgent, desperate quality drove Leo's life and work, and his poetry usually takes us to places we'd rather not go, places of almost unbearable pain. Time after time he strikes at the core of the human condition. As he speaks of his loss, he speaks of our loss as well, all loss. He drags us at a headlong pace down a hillside strewn with the rubble and thorns of doubt, self-pity, guilt, humiliation and self-punishment in his search for—what? Salvation? Redemption? Peace? At the very least, some closure?

> Father' we'll meet again.
> You can tell me you love me then.
> Mother, you have always been lost to me.
> I hope there comes a time
> when the game's over
> and I can see you....
> life ends and you
> become mine forever in among
> you and those you always wished
> to be with forever....

And then, ambivalence: "Mother, would/ it be better if we never met?" For:

> ... I was not always the good
> boy I have always believed you asked me to be,
> there are those who would tell you that I am not
> now a real man...

Could it be that all that's gone wrong is really *his* fault? And how could there possibly be a heaven? What form would it take?

> ...a lovely meadow green,
> sunshine happy forever, forgetting that
> here on earth we leave our paradisical
> vacations worn out, tired of the beach,
> weary of our last resort, back to rush and struggle...

But even in the midst of this doubting, he clings to a poignant hope:

> Mother, Father,
> I hope you are there when the moon dips low
> and I catch my ride... when the sweet scent
> of Maine is just caught where my breath ends.

Leo was often gruff and coarse and socially inept. He was also funny, compassionate and sensitive. Too sensitive for the rough fishing town of Rockland, Maine, where he grew up. Where his father, like most of the men in the town, respected hard physical work and athletics and money and not much else, certainly not poetry. In one of his poems he says that Maine

> ...ignores, betrays, kills its own; makes
> us feel, though Maine cannot provide for its bright youth,
> that we need an invisible passport if we leave, to
> come back... If you're from Maine
> your heart is here but nothing for you.

To a great extent, Leo was stuck in a time and place that no longer exists. Soon after he got out of high school—the same school the artist Louise Nevelson attended—he, like Nevelson, left Maine never to return except for brief visits. For over fifty years he continued to feel that Maine had nothing for him. But during those many years of self-exile, his hometown of Rockland, "Lime City," changed almost beyond recognition. The sardine plants and other fish-related industries of Leo's youth are history. Rockland today is a town of windjammer cruises and galleries, museums and shops, a haven for artists, and the lobstermen that ply its waters make very good money indeed.

But the earth is the same, the rocks, the sky, and the look and smell of the sea. And while there might be no heaven, maybe there could be Maine again, Leo thought—a Maine that in recent years had asked him to read at its colleges, had given him an honorary doctorate, a Maine that—he hoped—respected him.

The last time I saw him, in Rockland, four months before his death, he said to me, "In a few more years I'll stop working. Maybe then, I'll come home."

The Poetry of Leo Connellan

Emily Grosholz

Leo Connellan won my respect long ago by his devotion to the art of poetry, and in the intervening years by his decision to stay sober and take care of his family. When I first met him, he was still drinking and so was often difficult to deal with, but his poetry (and his faith in the power of art) were so moving that we all tried hard to accommodate him. He in turn was touched by our support and friendship, and returned it by sound and helpful advice, along with copies of his books and poems.

In the late 1970s, I ran a weekly poetry series called "Down to Earth," named after the small health food restaurant in the red light district of New Haven where it was held. In my weekly struggle to organize the event and get the publicity out, I was aided by various friends: Cathy Iino, Eleni Fourtouni, Helen Tartar, Dana Gioia, Wally Swist, Don Faulkner, and Syd Lea. There was no budget; poets were paid only by the rather meager gate, a free dinner, and our appreciation. But since we were located in the corridor between New York, Hartford, and Boston, it was never hard to find poets, local or en passant, and Leo Connellan was one of the distinguished cast of characters who read there, loud enough to be heard above the clatter of silverware and crockery or the revving engines of passing motorcycles. Given Leo's imposing presence and resonant Irish style of declaiming his poems that did full justice to their obsessive clarity, he never failed to rise above the surrounding noise.

Over the years, Leo and I kept in touch by telephone and letter, and I enjoyed a visit with him in 1993 at the Wesleyan Writers Conference. We traded poems back and forth; his red pencil, a poetic Occam's razor, always swept out the same admonition: pare it down! Under the compression of this severe economy, Leo's own poetry often ended up with highly non-standard arrangements of words, which nonetheless worked successfully for him. Over the years, I've wondered about this characteristic syntactical distortion of his, and offer my thoughts about it now, although he is no longer around to endorse or contest them. In the poetry of Leo Connellan, it seems to me, the distinction between nouns and verbs is undermined.

A feature of late 20th century American writer's workshop poetry is the overuse of gerunds, the formation that turns a verb into a noun by tacking on "ing." This habit mostly underscores a Heracleitean, "process" view of reality where everything runs, melting into the Flow with which we are expected to Go. Leo's poetry, conversely, fixes process or development and makes it look like a thing, frozen, I would say, by his obsessive art. He often employs a noun as a verb; puts a verb in a syntactical context where it may also be read as a noun; uses sentence fragments where the main verb never appears; uses a transitive verb without ever supplying an object; or forces transitive and intransitive verbs to do each other's work. At some deep level, Leo believed that nothing ever did change, so the best one could do was to face the changeless things and make them into poems. Some of his strongest writing, his most memorable verses, has this aspect of fixity: the dead leaf, the statue, the cadaver, ice. Fixity is the truth hiding behind the appearance of change.

Life

It's over,
smell, roses sweet, sweet
corn, the breath of breezes.
We lie unable to move
in dark grave where
there are no thrills
or they throw us ashes
that go nowhere yet all over
but is not seed.

(*Provincetown* 53)

Many of Leo's poems include the kind of vocative usually reserved for the dead in an elegy, but turned backwards and inwards to address himself, to assert in the midst of a meditation on the finality of death that he is still here. "I'm not dead!" as he wrote to me so often in his letters. Those poems, those letters, now have a pathos and irony about them, which I wonder if Leo foresaw. The poem "Life" does have two main verbs, but they express only passivity, an endless state: "it's over," and "we lie." The poem "Autumn" manages not to have any main verbs at all:

Autumn
Brown, brown leaves,
brown strangled orange.
Brown orange stiff turned in cold air
to crumble and disappear.
Cider scent on the wind
blowing its breath on mud ruts
into congealed reflections
holding summer for a look.
(*New and Collected Poems* 91)

Likewise, the opening of the poem "Garbage Truck" has no main verb, unless "come" is an imperative, but the opening line counts against that reading because of the strongly suggested parallel between "man built" and "scavenger come," so that "come" functions as a past participle leading into the next line.

Man built scavenger come
at firing squad time, the
low time of morning
when we most need to be loved
lest we rave our streets screaming
from the piled up truth....
(*The Maine Poems* 105)

The other candidate for the verb of the sentence is "rave," but it is tucked away in a subordinate clause and, though an intransitive verb, forced to take "streets" as its object. The result is a forcefully achieved moment of nightmare: just when we most need to sleep, to be comforted by a dream of love, the garbage truck thunders past. But the force of the poem is that it always thunders; we are trapped forever in the nightmare, at the coldest and darkest hour, just before dawn. The personification of such nightmare moments is the ghost, the revenant doomed to repeat the same cry or gesture of despair over and over, in a prison of attic, graveyard, or motel room, the place of its undoing. Leo's poems are full of ghosts, living and dead. So the poem "Stockbridge, Massachusetts" describes not an event but a place, a Red Lion Inn which has added modern wings to an eighteenth century core, haunted, of course, by someone: who is it? Perhaps a local spirit. "The carpeted rooms creak and their / carpets and fixtures suggest and hint trails you / traveled...." Perhaps the poet, perhaps the reader. "Beautiful in the Berkshires where / ice sparkles on tree branches when light rain freezes / and what is vanished is visible but the light of candles / flickering imagination is now electricity...." The wrenching of an intransitive verb from its normal function so as to take an object makes it less verb-like, assimilates it to the subject or object: the carpets and fixtures hint trails, the light of candles flickers imagination. Reading the poem, we are trapped in a hotel room populated by things, furniture and carpets, hypostatized hints and imagination, ghosts, with whom the poet identifies us (and himself).

> Now in our hustle
> and clatter we pay for creaks when we walk across rooms
> off balance as if creaking unites us with those whose
> breath breathed in these rooms which now heave from
> hanging on, shifted in this ancient building by rage
> of wind and storm....
>
> (*Provincetown* 20-21)

There is a main verb here in the welter of clauses: "we pay."

Leo Connellan has written heroically about the life of fishermen, their wives, their children, in the Rockland, Maine of his childhood in the 1930's, the Great Depression. It was a life trapped by poverty and violence, just as surely as the lobster and cod were trapped by the fishermen in pots and nets. In one sense, Leo escaped that world, by becoming a well-published poet, a teacher, and Poet Laureate of Connecticut. In another sense, as he tells us over and over in his poetry, he never did. His memories (and hardships) kept him fixed in that time and place, a revenant no matter how far he wandered, to San Francisco and New York City, with the ghosts of Federico Lorca and Jack Kerouac. But those memories, hammered into poems, are not merely personal, but social and ultimately artful. He re-creates not only his own loss and trauma, but that of a whole town of people trapped on the economic as well as the terrestrial margins of America. And he turns that re-creation into art, not so much a redemption or prayer as pure testimony: I am here. We are here. And we will continue to haunt you.

Reading Leo

Constance Hunting

When I read, silently, Leo Connellan's poems, I seem to hear his actual voice—pungent, truculent, yet with a crooning wistful quality underneath, perhaps an Irish inheritance. Anyone who has been to a Connellan reading always hears his voice on the printed page.

The voice, then, dominant. In person, Leo appeared slightly taller than average, rotund, and gave the impression of being light on his feet. Like many large people, he might have been a good dancer. He seemed to roll a bit as he walked, like a sailor on a tilting deck or a boxer ready at any time to go into a feint. Tentatively commanding on a platform, in a room he was expressively expansionist. His clothes had the appearance of having been flung on, not necessarily out of carelessness but because he was already on his way somewhere else. But when he folded his overcoat and laid it across a chair, it was with the tender precision of a boy who has been brought up poor and taught to treat good hand-me-downs with respect.

Tentatively commanding: behind the sometimes blustery, often challenging platform manner lurked a lovely diffidence—less towards the audience than towards the poetry he had been vouchsafed by a power, a muse, an occasionally fickle but ultimately faithful Melpomene—for Leo was a poet of tragedy.

His archetypal poem is not "Amelia, Mrs. Brooks of My Old Childhood," or "Lobster Claw," or "In Lobster Night" ("In N'York, aincha!" / "Yes, I am." "Like hit?" "I miss / home." "Ayah, I know hit!."), but "Helpless, We Go Into This Ground, Helpless":

> . . . Helpless, we go into this ground, helpless
> each day packed against each other so that
> we always start off irritable
> at being tossed about thrown against strangers.

. . . Helpless, down in the ground, we are under
the earth now in company of people we don't
know. . . helpless into this ground, helpless.

As it is the mark of the lyric poet to hear music and that of the witty poet to see comedy in rue, so it is the habit of tragic poets to find death in a daily subway ride. The feeling of being helpless, without protection, dangerously close to hopelessness, doubtless sprang from Leo's ancestral and native sources, his double temperamental and geographic citizenship.

Portland and Rockland, Maine, out of Ireland's County Clare-to-America because "Jesus wouldn't make potatoes grow" was Leo's history, with all of its stereotypes intact, the gritty successful grandfather, his son spoiled by education, failure, and skewed hubris, his grandson wanting only to be himself, a poet:

. . . I was violated in my boyhood
by the tip of your forelock terror
fear, my parents' fear of their jobs,
place in the community if any
child of theirs tried to become
a Poet or Ballerina or Actress.
(from "The Moon Now Flushed")

If Leo's feet are perforce on the ground, his head is in the lowering clouds. Rarely does his consciousness enjoy a respite from its rage and pity. Yet these emotions are shot through by rays of remarkable clarity. That's right, we feel; Leo's got it. In some respects his poetry reminds of the Canadian Al Purdy's, also a maverick but one who looked outward with fewer inner complications. "Who do you think you are?" is a key Maine question at a broad level of the culture:

Who did you think you were'!' . . .

Screamed into you and
Broke you, broke your heart
Broke your ambitions, your
initiative and made you
overweight or in a hospital
or in drink. . . . .
(from "The Moon Now Flushed")

And Leo's been in all three situations; Leo's got it. Any reluctant society in the country, perhaps in the human world, partakes of the peck-to-death order of the barnyard.

So what were Leo's defenses?

First, of course, his talent. It will not, cannot be gainsaid. Second, his anger, fuel for the poetry, its sensibility and intonation; and for his psychic life. Mixed with this anger, twisting through it as it were, is the double thread of (unwarranted) loathing of self and self-indulgence which lead to the characteristic attitude he shared with his father: "I must be appeased!" Leo's technique is usually that of speech intensified, amplified to a Lear-like level. And yet Connellan—his third defense—is for the most part in complete control of his craft. Although he generally eschews received form, he does not eschew pattern. At times, however, sound seems to matter less to him than fury.

His designated masterpiece is the trilogy, *The Clear Blue Lobster-Water Country.* Book I, "Coming to Cummington to Take Kelly," is perhaps less successful than the others, less overtly wrought; but always a sort of sly intelligence is at work, at once revealing and concealing. The play on "Coming" and "Cummington" is echoed by the play on "Kelly" and "Kelley" in the body of the book; but even as the young narrator is puzzled by the coincidence of the names of the summer camp torturer and the exemplary Boston sports figure, the reader shares the slight discomfort at the homophonic ploy. Like the boy, the reader goes back and forth between the names; but literally, on the page. The boy intuits the confusion between good and evil, the reader understands the symbolic combination.

The text of "Coming to Cummington" is presented in short sharp bursts of pain:

> Your life was
> disappointed in guilt
> from birth to hesitate,
> scream at everyone like
> anyone suddenly grabbed
> and held and branded
> not only white-hot flesh
> but deep within.

The piston-like rhythm is all, form, rhyme, other poetic devices subsumed in the technique of pain. The repeated "Father"—"I write it for you, Father," "my / love of you, Father," "Father, I have to say it"—is like the prayerful address of his Catholic childhood, even dropping occasionally into "Daddy," the "Abba" of the New Testament ("Daddy do you remember"). Here too is introduced the Boppledock figure, "Bop" in the later trilogy poems, who is cousin to Berryman's "Henry" in his dream poems, a somewhat *commedia dell'arte* or Pulcinella figure, loose-jointed and irresponsible whom Connellan is partial to as a relief from his tormented self.

Book II of this poetic triptych, "Shatterhouse," which in 1982 won the Shelley Memorial Award, after the familiar conversational beginning, is more formally ordered, with approximately 130 stanzas of twelve lines each piled like building blocks towards the father's "unfulfilled / wish to become again the original and to/make a future, your wildest imagining!" The mother is also called upon ("Mother, we'll meet again./ I will tell you I love you then") though not with a clearly Biblical connection; so that these parents, disallowed compatibility by circumstance and place, are brought together but never reconciled by their hopeful, despairing poet-son.

Book III, whose title is that of the trilogy, shows Connellan at the top of his form. The section is at once divided and sustained by its thirty sections of three-line stanzas which remind of one of Williams' favorite "modes of attack." In this final part, Connellan's voice is less frantic though of course never entirely calm. "Bop" comes into his own as a real character, not a caricature. And there is a Mrs. Bop; and their child Lollipop. Connellan has caught the echo of Bop's voice mingled with Rockland, Maine's: "no furrener better think he cummin' inta th'clear/blue lobster-water country-n-take a payday/from any real American"; "I was over to th'university because / Lollipop told me I ought t'learn more / 'bout different worlds, not // be a Boppledock all m'life!" Such transcription is not only colored by the local but has the effect of being dragged up from its own underground of deep, puzzled silence. But also the poem's language can turn beautiful, high, classical and romantic:

Once I would have caught your breath for you!
What lasts longer, the knotty thick tree
or fleeting wildflower that stirs
your blood . . . .

I love you in your acorn hair still
fresh from country hay and lust . . . .

Oh I have looked
like death, lady, for a long time now

layers of age over youth, glass windows
over eyes desiring . . . .

Finally, Bop dies ("Feeling himself / lifted now, Bop / closed his eyes"), leaving his creator both free and fettered. Free of the enormous task the trilogy represented, and fettered by the need to write, always, more.

Leo Connellan is in the tradition of Wordsworth who wished to write in the language "really spoken by men" and to direct his attention to the "knowledge which all men carry about with them, and to sympathies in which, without any other discipline than that of our daily life, we are fitted to take delight." Delight! Judging from the general run of his poetry, if he recognized delight, might easily spurn it. "Rage, rage" is more in his line, and lines. And yet—is the rant and rage leading somehow to the courage to write ("Write it!") the sweetness and sadness which is not nostalgia but, simply, love?

Blueberry Boy

I only wish I could have it just once more,
you go back and the place looks dull and
small in its mosquito biting green.
I was a Blueberry boy in that childhood,
the sun would flush my freckles out
from where winter hid them in the
sallow pale color of snow and I would
run the meadow for blueberries that
my aunt Madge would turn into muffins

> I have longed for down the tripup of manhood.
> Just a minute again, on my knees, picking
> frantically with expert watered tongue,
> ignorant of what lay out of the woods.

In *On the Nature of the Universe,* Lucretius writes:

> In those creatures whose passionate hearts and choleric dispositions easily boil up in anger, there is a surplus of the hot element. An outstanding example is the truculent temper of lions, who often roar till they burst their chests with bellowing and cannot keep the torrents of their rage pent within.

Leo was well-named. But sometimes the lion lies blinking in the sun.

"Whereas Leo...": A Reminiscence on the Late Poet Laureate

Sydney Lea

I first met Leo Connellan in 1976, when Richard Eberhart, the dean of poetry at Dartmouth, where I then taught, invited him to read under the auspices of a fund set up by Dick's wonderful wife Betty. Betty, an heir to the Butcher Wax fortune, deserves her own essay, as dear Leo, were he living today, would surely agree. She trod her own path as much as Leo himself ever did. A Boston Brahmin, still she was open to anything, and she lived for the new. To that extent, Betty's motive in establishing the so called Butcher Fund at Dartmouth was to bring to attention the work of writers who had not yet carved out a reputation, who had published one book or even none.

Leo was in fact one of three male writers to read on the Butcher-Funded occasion I'm recalling. At 46, he was really of another generation from his two nonce colleagues. Each of them had a book out at the time, whereas Leo was still awaiting his first full volume, which, not so oddly, would be a first selected poems.

I'd be more forgiving now, but in 1976 I was only 33 years old myself, and it seemed to me that the preening and the posturing and the ever so cultivated elegance of the two other writers, neither of whose names I'll mention here, were the sort of stuff that gives poets a bad name. It is perhaps significant that I haven't heard or read a word by or about these two young men since, whereas Leo....

It was always "Whereas Leo" for me, even when he was whining at me, or was angry, or was just full of shit, as he, like anyone, could be.

Whereas Leo kept right on trucking to the last breath. His drive to do so, even when he was without portfolio, so to speak, was what set him apart from and above those other two men. This capacity to keep at it, to be a poet no matter what, is the trait in this quirky, often difficult, always passionate man that lodged in my mind then, abides there still, and—when as poet or human being I tend to get whiny myself—serves as a tonic and a corrective.

Yes, he kept at it to the last breath.

Indeed, it was a line containing that word, "breath," that above all stopped me in my tracks that evening. It stopped a lot of people. The famous pin would have resounded in the big hall had it been dropped there then:

You couldn't catch your breath for her.

That's the very end of Leo's "Old Orchard Beach Burned Down," one of his earlier efforts but still one of his most poignant and deft. In that poem, the author's reminiscence on Old Orchard Beach as a sort of fantasy land, the realm of wonder and magic and inexplicable excitement, is likened to a young love now turned old and cronish but still in memory the sinecure of everyone's eye—especially Leo Connellan's.

It was not just the absolute accuracy and adequacy of that close that made everyone else breathless too; it was the way in which Connellan breathlessly intoned it, gave it a sort of physical existence that ranged among us, and suggested, like everything else he rendered that night, the badge of commitment and passion that I've alluded to.

I heard that line, *felt* that line, turned to my colleague Jay Parini and uttered: "Jesus, that's the real stuff."

I'd never experienced the real stuff live before.

Leo Connellan, for much of his youth and middle age, was, as he openly admitted, a drunk, even at times a hobo. Bad luck followed him, precisely in the manner that—never mind the mindless saw about God's looking out for drunks and Irishmen—bad luck follows the addict.

When I heard Leo read at Dartmouth, for instance, he was keeping sober for a spell, making his living as a salesman. Of what? Well, as it happens, of carbon paper, typewriter ribbons—that sort of thing. While in Hanover, like any good salesman he'd made a contact or two, so that in less than a full week after the reading I saw him schmoozing with the English department secretary, whom he successfully convinced to buy a load of these office supplies. We exchanged pleasantries and good wishes, he left, and I remarked that an order from the department must be a sort of bonanza for him.

The secretary, a genuinely good and kind woman, wistfully replied: "Perhaps, but that will be the last order he does get from us."

"Why's that?"

"Everyone's getting one of those new Xerox contraptions, including us."

Leo was a topnotch salesman of office supplies, the sort that were just about to go the way of the dodoes.

Bad luck. There was plenty of it, not all of which I'm at liberty to mention.

Leo was shortly enough laid off, of course, and another round of troubles began for him, culminating in the rehab stay he so searingly memorialized in his *Clear Blue Lobster-Water Country* trilogy, the second part of which, "Shatterhouse," remains as compelling a portrait of that sort of institutionalization as I know, far wiser and less ego-driven, say, than Berryman's *Recovery.*

Berryman, tragically, leapt from that bridge in Minnesota, whereas Leo...

Whereas Leo kept on keeping on. Indeed, after his stay at what he acidly refers to as Little Hope Hospital, Connellan never took another hit of alcohol nor of any substitute. He made his way, though it was not always easy. He was unduly ashamed of the fact that he never earned a college degree, and unjustly (or only semi-justly) ascribed his under-recognition to that lacuna. By dint of persistence, however, he became the poet at large for the Connecticut state university system, taking his passion and intelligence and talent into all manner of venues, chiefly secondary school classrooms; and at the end he was poet laureate of his adopted Connecticut. Before he died, he had earned several honorary doctorates.

He gave me far too much credit for supporting him. I'd done no more than to publish a fair amount of his poetry in my capacity as founder and editor of *New England Review*. As I told him, and told him genuinely, I took the poems for the same reason I took other people's poems: they were good. At their best, they were damned good. And I was pleased to forge a relationship, editor to poet, poet to poet, that would survive so long as Leo survived. In a sense, it survives even now. He's with me.

Looking back on it now, after the pain of his loss had subsided in me some, I can say that he had a distinguished career, no doubt about it, though his own doubts would never fully ebb. No accolade—not even the doctorates, not even the coveted Shelley Memorial Award from the Poetry Society of America—fundamentally changed him. He remained, in all candor, a crank, and that could grate on one. No one has ever kept me on the telephone as long and as often as he did, and by way of consolation to myself at his passing, I thought, Well, I'll have a big chunk of non-Leo time on my hands now. Who could have guessed—not me—that I'd actually miss his rants and rambles and good talk and all the rest?

One thing's for sure: Leo Connellan, even as his reputation and his job security waxed, never became an "academic" writer. He couldn't have done that had he been called forth by Oxford or the Sorbonne, had someone held two shotguns to his head. Deep in his blood was the notion that poetry was not only an art but also a way of life, an attitude toward the world. You had to work at being a poet, and for him that meant going to places where many of us poets don't go. If he was in Provincetown, he scouted for the ghosts of the hardscrabble fishermen who, unlike now, once populated that beautiful but harsh coign.

If he found himself staying overnight on the road, he was sensitive to the lives and trials of the chambermaids and busboys.

He was a man, after all, who knew what it was to sleep in the weeds. He'd done all manner of what we euphemistically call odd jobs. The hard-pressed hiree who changes his bed in a Motel looks at him—and Leo knows she sees their commonalty.

I had a lot in common with Leo too, but it wasn't of that sort. I have taught all my adult life in toney private colleges. Dartmouth. Wesleyan. Yale. Middlebury (I may even have been an "academic" writer myself now and then; I hope not, but I'm not the one to judge.) But since I first met him, I've had Leo on my shoulder at all of those places. In my teaching and in my writing, I can hear him whispering. He says what the hip-hop artists of a later day keep saying: Keep it real.

And so many of my pampered students (and a disarming number of their professors) attempt to do just that. How? Well, they think they speak for, and they claim to champion, the oppressed, the proletarian, and so on. Trouble is, they have no means of doing so: to write of such matters is, in effect, to write about the world that they know least. And I always use Leo as an example of one who has, in the dread buzz phrase of our time, "Been there, done that." He never urged me nor anyone—in the interest of keeping it real—to live the life that he had lived. No, he was merely holding up a standard of honesty that I think we all can benefit by meeting.

His rule, as I recall, was something like this: Don't bullshit anyone.

Good advice. Bullshit is not only an aesthetic dead end but it's also somehow morally repugnant for tenured members of such and such an English department to be writing poems about gang life, say, their research based, after all, on ... what? Reading? What they see spray-painted on walls from the windows of their railroad cars or their automobiles as they make their way to class or to the faculty meeting? And the same goes for their students. Leo is, as I say, ever helpful to me as I try to make such a point in my own classes and meetings.

And, needless to say, I have small patience with the Ivy-bedecked student or teacher-writer who complains of busy-ness, of all the pressures that conspire to keep him or her from writing more and better. Leo, "Crossing America," was essentially a bindle stiff and a barfly—and he kept on writing. The poems kept coming.

Don't bullshit anyone, I think.

Don't bullshit yourself above all, I think.

These days I may be driving more than I'm writing, with kids all over the map in their disparate schools out here in the woods; I might complain of how all this gets in the way of my poetry, whereas Leo....

Whereas Leo would do any last thing he had to do to keep a roof over himself and his excellent wife Nancy and his daughter Amy. And to keep the poems pouring forth. Right to the last breath.

He was and is a model.

Ave atque vale.

Learning from Leo

Sheila A. Murphy

After his appointment as Connecticut's Poet Laureate in 1996, Leo said, "The most important thing, for me, is to help young people. God has been kind enough to give me a little notice and attention, and I want to pass on something." How many miles, I wonder, did Leo drive in that precarious old car, in his quest to pass on a passion for poetry to Connecticut students? And how many students' and teachers' voices were enriched by his voice and presence? My memories stem from the five years, 1994 through 1999, when Leo visited my classes in Glastonbury High School.

"Everything I'm going to tell you is wrong," Leo would begin, savoring a prolonged pause as his eyes worked the room, "but it is right for me." My recollections only hint at the ways Leo's voice continues to reverberate. That salesman voice blended with the voice of his poems, surrounding poems with his love of language, his thirst for knowledge, and his compassion for suffering humanity. Teenage voices, too, conjure Leo, in the ways that my students reacted to him and learned from him. Finally, my own voice, as teacher and learner, reminds me of the ways our relationship grew.

I had never heard of Leo Connellan when his friend Gary McManus, a guidance counselor, urged me to invite Leo to my Advanced Composition class. Gary knew that my "Writers on Writing" unit included inviting guest writers to discuss their craft. I was hesitant but took home the book Gary offered. That night I read *The Clear Blue Lobster-Water Country* at one sitting, mesmerized by its harsh cadences. The next day, the first of many long and rambling phone conversations with Leo convinced me that this poet would be a risky but worthwhile guest.

I wondered, though, whether my affluent suburban students would relate as I had to those raw vignettes of struggling Maine lobstermen, cannery workers, and descendents of Irish immigrants (like Leo, and me). Eventually, I would invite Leo to teach in all my classes, advanced to remedial sections, in grades 9 through 12. His bluster and name-dropping could seem like braggadocio, but a curious vulnerability hovered beneath the surface. "Was I all right?" he would ask as students left for their next class.

Leo became a familiar and colorful presence at our rather conventional school. Ever the salesman, he would be one of the first in the school, appearing an hour before the opening bell rang. I would arrive to find Leo chatting with an administrator, secretary, or custodian—whoever happened to be in the office.

I learned to fetch Leo a cup of black coffee to jump-start his day while he waited in our English workroom for classes to begin. He would rail at world news, bristle at overheard profanities, and scowl at the occasional student with green spiked hair (a small but visible minority in a Gap-clad student body). Eventually, students, teachers and staff became used to Leo following me down a crowded hallway between classes. Once, after hearing Leo pontificate on the state of the world, on teenage wardrobes, and on the poetry establishment, a colleague watched as I maneuvered Leo toward another classroom. "You looked like a lion-tamer," he remarked, "trying to control an unpredictable beast, obviously fond of him, and respecting him, but not sure of what he would do next."

What Leo did next was surprise and beguile my students, whatever the class, whatever the achievement level, and whatever their initial interest in poetry (which tended to be minimal). Leo's physical appearance was the first surprise for students. "He didn't look like a poet!" was a refrain I heard after his first visit. One student wrote: "His appearance startled me. I had expected a rugged looking man, dressed in khakis and a faded polo. When he spoke, I expected a highly-educated sounding tone with well-pronounced words forming themselves into profound phrases with varied meanings. Instead he was a cartoon-like man in a plaid shirt and green tie, with a Maine-New England accent."

Leo's words soon won over students who had preconceived notions of what a poet should look like. Another student wrote: "I feel that his voice is perfect. It's rough and raspy. ...I learned so much in a short period of time." One student summarized Leo's visits aptly: "He made me laugh, and taught me to read deeper, but more simply, into poems."

Leo put students at ease with his self-deprecating humor. Humor was a seamless part of his performance. Delivered deadpan but with a twinkle in his eye, his one-liners would loosen up poetry-wary teenagers:

> "First there was the wheel, then there was projected light, then I was born."
>
> "You don't have to be afraid of me. I can wiggle my ears" (demonstrating same).
>
> "I'm deaf in one ear, and can't hear in the other."

After a 1998 visit, one student remarked: "He seemed, although he was old certainly, to be able to connect with high-schoolers. He made jokes a lot which helped dispel the aura of elite intellectualism which my mind connects with poets in general." Leo knew that if students became comfortable with him, they might become comfortable with poetry.

Leo did captivate students with his knowledge, but his convoluted style of delivery was sometimes confusing. His comments could stray far from the poem students were looking at. Once, a student asked a straightforward question about a poet's reputation. What followed next was a long discourse about how Robert Browning was derided for his poem "Sordello" (not the poem students had read). Then, thinking aloud, he continued, "He was married to a beautiful woman. Her father never spoke to her after they were married. Elizabeth Barrett's poem 'How do I love thee?' is one of the most beautiful love poems in the English language." Without a pause, he added, "I started to receive some recognition in 1983... took me 53 years." Finally, he would answer the student's question. As a fan of poems by both the Brownings, I found his comments enlightening. For students, though, they were a distraction. His inimitable style and racing mind sometimes precluded brevity, and, alas, clarity.

During a first visit, Leo would write on the chalkboard: *A poem creates an image and then stops. A story has to tell it all.* That maxim was central. Leo would weave it into discussions about his own poems, and about poems by others. He focused on concepts such as *image* and *allusion* to help students understand the compression and precision of poetic language. In deciding on poems for classroom use, I would ask Leo to choose whatever poems he wanted to use. One favorite was his poem "To War Dead." After reading this poem, he would help students understand *allusion* by reciting the World War I poem, "In Flanders Fields," to show its connection to his war poem. (The first time Leo recited that poem, in a solemn tone, he brought tears to my eyes, as my mother's voice, reciting those same words decades ago, echoed in my memory.)

"I paid homage to Colonel McCrae," Leo would say. "That's what poets do...." Pointing out the images of flowers and war in both poems, he would ask: "How does Leo Connellan create a machine gun image? By creating an image that *you* can see—*Leaves of you young flowers fall/ like shook horse-chestnut trees.*" Then Leo couldn't resist a mini-lecture. He'd ask students, "What is the worst thing war can do?" searching until he received the answer he wanted—"The worst thing war can do is kill your progeny." He would urge: "Be the best that you can be—whoever the foe is... sometimes ourselves," a comment that probably resonated more strongly with me than with teenagers.

Sometimes Leo would mention poets without reading their work: "This is why we read. Something happened before you got here. Before I got here." He would name Walt Whitman when questions surfaced, as they always did, about the issue of poems that do not rhyme. "Time goes on," Leo would begin. "Rhymes were invented to carry messages. Fifteen hundred years ago, at night, no cars, no lights. People couldn't travel. They wrote in rhymes, forms. They wrote poems to carry messages."

Whitman, said Leo, wrote "lyric narrative verse. It changed poetry. I have done my work in the time I have lived in." He talked of learning from Whitman that "You don't have to rhyme if you can create an image with meter in the line." Once, illustrating "meter in the line," he read a line from his poem "Snowflake," ever so slowly: *wa - ter - we - have - sunk - in - holds - us - up*. For me, having students learn from a poet about Whitman's contribution to American poetry trumped any textbook explanation of free verse.

The need for revision was another of Leo's lessons. Many students vehemently resist the idea of revising poems. "The poet who succeeds knows that most of what he writes he cannot use.... throw it away," was a vivid reminder that poetry is craft as well as art. After that lesson an aspiring poet wrote: "The fact that he must think about what he is writing, as opposed to everything being inspiration, gives me hope for my own writing."

"Scott Huff" was a perennial favorite in all classes. Obviously, most teenagers could identify with the story of a young man their age, working late to earn money for college, who fell asleep at the wheel, and died in a single car accident. "I tried to create the real loss of Scott Huff—by creating those images [*yellow buttercups/salmon for my heart in the rivers/ fresh springs of ice cold water running away*] so you could see the real loss of Scott Huff," Leo told students. To underscore Leo's point about images, I "expanded" that poem for students into a long prose story that did indeed "tell it all"—and, inevitably, destroyed the poem. When Leo saw what I had done, he liked the way students could see, in contrast, the precision, compression, and music of his poem.

When questions arose about where poems come from, Leo would answer with a story. Once he described helping his wife Nancy deliver Avon products in Clinton, Connecticut, and an encounter with one of her regular customers: "This woman—she had to be seventy if she was a day—said she wanted to get back to Rockland, Maine. 'I need to move back,' she said. 'I have to get to my son. I'm not sure he can survive the death of his son.'" Leo would pause again, before saying: "And then I tried to create the real loss of Scott Huff—by creating those images—so you could see the real loss of Scott Huff." To learn about the art and craft of poetry through the eyes of a gifted practitioner was memorable and instructive for us all.

Students often chafed at the serious topics that dominate Leo's poems. Once a student asked: "Do you have happy poems?" Leo's response was that he wrote about "things that disturb us... things that need change." His poems memorialize the human struggle to survive, and to find meaning in life. In one of his last poems, Leo again gave me his response to something that disturbed him, and me. In May, 1998, my grandson died, at eleven months, of a genetic disease, Spinal Muscular

Atrophy. "There just isn't anything I can say," Leo muttered (for once at a loss for words), and then he hung up abruptly.

Two weeks later, I heard his brusque voice on the phone at school: "How do you pronounce your grandson's name?" And then: "Do you have a minute? I want to read you something. The title is 'My Messenger.'" I listened to this poem:

Cianan DeWeer Murphy
You know the wind now all its whispers.
And the sun that blinds me are your eyes.
You were here to forgive me, my
rough youth's wild crime, for
as life vanishes, you live, forever.
Tell God I am not lying when I
say I'm sorry, I'm a coward
and afraid, but not lying.

As with "Scott Huff," written decades earlier, the death of a young person had had led to a brief, arresting poem. Two years later, Leo called to tell me that "My Messenger" would be published in the *Puckerbrush Review*. Today, that poem, typed and autographed, is framed in my home, beside a picture of my grandson. Another copy hangs in my son's home.

Leo's visits to my classes resonate more vividly than many of my other teaching experiences. He introduced poems with bluster and wisdom and wit, nurturing a love for poetic rhythms and ideas, for craft and art. In 1994, I hoped this new acquaintance might win over students to poetry. I could not know that I would become the student most changed by Leo. Our teaching collaboration ended with my retirement in 1999, but our friendship endured, and his influence continues. The harsh cadences and rough grace of his poetry echo whenever I read, write, or meditate on poetry.

Editor's note:
The late William Packard's comments in the "Special Featured Poet: Leo Connellan" section of *Negative Capability* (1994) serve here to introduce Packard's interview of Leo from *The Poet's Craft: Interviews from The New York Quarterly* (1987).

LEO CONNELLAN: ENORMOUS HEART AND SOUL

William Packard

Since 1970 when we began *The New York Quarterly* magazine, we've probably given more page space to Leo Connel1an than to any other contemporary American poet. "Violent Dying," "Lament For Federica Garcia Lorca," "Shadows," "The Moon Now Flushed"—they were long poems and took up a large part of each issue. But we knew they were worth it. Another thing: over the past 20+ years, I can't recall ever rejecting any of Leo Connellan's work that he sent on to me—not once. He'd send a manuscript of a new poem, and we'd take it. Now that probably says more about Leo than it does about us—he wasn't into making fancy multiple submissions, and he didn't arrange a pretty bouquet so if the lead poem didn't grab you in all its raw violence and voice and power, there'd be three or four other wee poems you could choose from. Leo wasn't that kind of poet. He put his enormous heart and soul into every poem he wrote, at enormous risk, and the results show. No wonder we took each and every poem Leo Connellan ever sent us. And we're proud we did.

The Poet's Craft: Interview Number 24— Leo Connellan

William Packard

Q: *I've been reading through all your poems. And, there are so many long poems which, usually, are seen by poets as a challenge. When did you start writing long poems?*

A: When I was very young I wanted to be, if possible, a short story writer like Stephen Crane and I couldn't do it. No matter how I tried, it didn't come out. So, I tried writing novels and every other thing and they didn't come out and after a long time, I began to try to see if I could write poetry. But in the beginning, in the early 1960s, it was an accomplishment if I could get off the page. It was an accomplishment. It was really—I wrote a poem called "Lament for Federico Garcia Lorca" that runs about two and a half pages and to me it was an achievement that I could actually write what I thought was a poem that long.

Q: *Let me ask you a question about that poem. That poem ends:*

> *Federico, Garcia, Lorca ...some of us*
> *some of us are heartbroken . . .*
> *They do not make enough candles*
> *in all the world's churches*
> *to burn for you.*
> *Not enough Rosaries can be said*
> *or Acts of Contrition.*
> *Because I know*
> *it will happen again.*

You seem to have a great talent for talking directly to a subject or to the reader. Are you aware of doing this?

A: Not consciously. No. But in writing poems, one of the things that I've tried to do is read it silently to myself as if it were being read to me so I could try to understand it. And if I can't seem to understand what I thought I've gotten on paper, then I try to make what it is "clear for me;" if it's clear to me it may be clear to you. . .It's a device I've tried to perfect.

Q: *Does that get into revising endlessly?*

A: I didn't revise. For me the thing that defeats people who say they want to write is not realizing that writing is work! You have to write everything out. Everything about whatever it is you want to write. Even if doing it will fill 100 pages. Knowing you may only be able to use half a page. I seldom revise. If I get to the point where I think through that process of writing every single thing out about a poem and the poem is finished, then what I do is edit, edit, edit, cut, edit, cut again. But once I've done that, I never touch the poem again. ..for any reason. Now for instance, I wrote a poem that the *NYQ* published called "The Moon Now Flushed" and I wrote a poem called "Portrait of a Poet." I wouldn't touch these poems. I'm an older person now, a different person. They were written twenty years ago. But when they were delivered to the editor, or to the world, they were and are in the best shape that I would ever be able to make them. Revising them now would be breaking faith with one's development. They are what I was and what I wrote when I wrote them. Now that I might know more does not give me a right to cheat art and who I was then and am now.

Q: *You also wrote a poem "Watching Jim Shoulders." It seems like some of the poems are searching for a hero of some kind. Are you aware of that?*

A: Interesting you ask that. I have no conscious awareness of picking athletic heroes or picking heroes at all. I've had several periods in my life as a very heavy drinker. Once I was in Colorado Springs, Colorado as the guest of the Salvation Army and they got us indigents tickets to go see a rodeo. I went along to get along.... Someone I had never heard of suddenly came lunging out of a corral on the back of a steer, and somebody said it was somebody called Jim Shoulders who, even though he'd seriously hurt his back, was nevertheless riding that steer to keep his North America title for the United States. .. I saw a man who had seriously injured his back come out of a corral and throw a steer in a matter of seconds while blood squirted up his back; I saw him stand erect and walk back as if nothing was hurting him; and it suddenly occurred to me that I had to wonder: when did my manhood awaken to its whatever.... And, later, years later in New York City, I'd come down into Greenwich Village and sat in The Limelight and things like "Watching Jim Shoulders" would occur to me to try to make into poems.

Q: *O.K. Of the long poems, "Lobster Claw," "In Lobster Night, "Coming to Cummington to Take Kelly," "Crossing America"—many of these poems start with someone coming into a town or coming back to a town, or like environment, dying, leaving the town. Exits and entrances seem to be very important in the long poems.*

A: I'm not conscious of that. I'm conscious of a feeling that everyone is searching for who they are, where they are, whether they ever leave where they are or not. I come from New England. There are people in New England who never go five miles from where they were born and they are some of the most neurotic, frustrated, resentful, upset people I've ever met in my life. And they don't know why. They need you to come to spend your money, but they resent you for the ability to earn it somewhere else and, apparently, to be able to pay your bills and have enough left over. They need you to spend in their town but resent you for being able to—and I think I get a sense of displacement and I don't think I'm unique. I think Shakespeare certainly wrote from that point of view and most writers, many writers, are disturbed by the fact that there—as Hemingway said "There is no separate peace...."

Q: *You keep insisting that you are not conscious of certain things that I see in your work. What the hell are you conscious of when you're working? Are you thinking about line breakage? The way the poem falls on the page?*

A: No. That never bothers me at all.

Q: *What do you think about?*

A: I think about what I want to try to do with the poem. In other words, I make a plan. For example, in the poems that you mentioned, if I could write a poem about where I came from and the people, that would be a vantage point (or practice point) for me to try to do a body of work about my origins later on. Because I think of writing as, well, let me talk about me. I have to give myself permission to fail in order to succeed... as Yeats suggested. So first, before I try for my real work, my big effort, I have to try to write about little things I notice. So if I'm crossing America, I'll try to write about what I noticed about, say Kansas, or about hitchhiking, or if I go to New York City, I'll try to write about the Staten Island Ferry and the subway hoping the day will come when I have a right to write about my New England. Then, perhaps, I have the right to try to see what I think may bother human beings.... I think my subject matter better "move" me, "disturb" me or it's certainly not going to reach out and touch complete strangers and move them to consider what I'm writing about.

Q: *But you say you do throw away a lot?*
A: If you see a poem of mine that's twenty five pages long, you can rest assured that it was 200 pages long and the twenty-five pages, the final version, is edited, everything, everything written out about whatever it is I'm trying to write about, several times in pen and ink, all out—200 pages, finally everything thrown away but what can't be; then, maybe I've trapped my poem—maybe!

Q: *You type several drafts?*
A: No. I never type it until I'm ready to send it to a publisher. I never type it until the poem is written. The poem is written in pen and ink until it satisfies me. It may go through one draft—I carried the manuscript of *Crossing America* around with me for ten years, for example....I didn't even think it was a finished work....Another example is my book *Massachusetts Poems*; the Cummington poem was written in two months in a motel room that I lived in while at the company headquarters where I worked in Pinebrook, New Jersey....And up in Peabody, Massachusetts and wherever I happened to be as a traveling salesman making my living. I would go out all day and make my living as a salesman and come back into my hotel room and write, work!

Q: *You talk as if you were constantly at work on something. What is the longest period of dry that you've ever gone through, that you haven't been writing?*

A: Ah, it's very funny. I was dry probably from the time I was a young man, probably from 1947 through to about 1964. In other words, I had written some poems in high school, but no matter how many times I tried to get going I just couldn't do it. I couldn't do it in New York City, I couldn't seem to write when I was in various cities of the U.S. or Canada, and I sense that a lot of it, for me, had to do with the fact that I lived my adolescence probably between age twenty and thirty rather than between age twelve and twenty. Suddenly, when I married and came back to New York City in the early 1960s, a city, mind you, that loomed large in my head as a place I'd always failed in, I wasn't thinking in terms of "books" but of individual poems. Could I write one poem!? I mean I would go out and write a poem, and the big accomplishment of the month was if I had a poem half finished. And in that way, I wrote two books at the same time, I wrote *Another Poet in New York* and *Penobscot Poems* at the same time. If I got tired of writing about the New York subway system, I'd turn around and write about a Maine lobster fisherman.

Q: *You're talking about two kinds of geography—where you come from and where you are when you are writing the poem ....*

A: The city that I love and the state of Maine which is my origin seem to be basically what I write about or—a lot of my work when I was trying to teach myself to write was about Maine and New York.

Q: *Do you have any feelings of kinship with the other great Maine poets like Robinson, Coffin ... and who are the other Maine poets? Millay. Edna St. Vincent Millay ...Who else?*

A: Well, no. Millay, now you know, don't you, that Edna Millay and I both come from Rockland, Maine. ..let's see, I'll tell you something.... When I read your own plays *The Marriage,* and especially a work of yours like *My Name is Bobby*, it did far more for me, probably triggered some of my own guts to try to write my work, than any of these poets you've mentioned.... I don't think, I mean I think it sounds awfully nice to put yourself in a group like Robinson,

Frost, even the other sea poet Jeffers... but I'm, a loner. I'm so unrelated to them that I've never felt either involved with them or that I ever wrote anything because of them.... I owe you, Bill, and, say, Richard Wilbur, Federico Garcia Lorca poets of the world, if I owe anyone....which I hope I don't....

Q: *I'm going to read this poem—*
Through The World The Little Worm Forever

In blizzard at toll booth
trucks backed up like
empty egg crates, their
lights on in the snow falling linen dust
makes them look furious beetles
bright round large bulbous glazed eyes
dead or glaring, like giants
tied held prisoner, taunted,
by something that didn't occur to them possible.

All backed up the falling snow
flicked against trucks windshield glass
like feathers of cotton candy sticking
to windows like furry little hands it
takes scraping to get off. Cold sticking
and cunningly worked under their
big thick tires to skid them out of control.
through the world the little worm forever while
big species vanish, invisibility is power,
victory your opponent's ignorance.

That poem has such an extraordinary observed detail which is where in poetry of someone's actually re-creating the way those big trucks looked when they're backed up and the way the little snowflakes stick on the windshield. You say you did this in a motel room?

A: Yes.... I'll tell you something, too, and I'm not trying to impress you.... I just want you to see how I work. That poem is a practice poem, was written as a practice poem.

Q: *A practice poem?*

A: I was trying to develop the ability in sharp poetic sharp lines to describe something to help me get ready for the work I was writing at the time which was called "Coming to Cummington to Take Kelly" and I was about to try to take on a running scene, a scene of imagined action. So, in my room, I had the habit sometimes of writing what I call throwaway poems. Sometimes I'd send 'em out until I-'til somebody buys one for a magazine or even puts it in the little book that you noticed from Western Maryland Press.

Q: *Do you do these warm-up poems all the time?*

A: Constantly. When you asked me about dry periods, this is why it was hard for me to answer you literally because if I can't write what I do is practice. In the poem you read, my, "Through the World the Little Worm Forever," I was trying to work with the conclusion that sometimes one wins by being invisible and sometimes your victory is in your opponent's ignorance... meaning, too, that none of us are so "good that we can afford enemies. If I can't write what I do is practice, practice. I try to use myself every day. I get up every morning of my life, nobody asks me to. And I'm certainly not suggesting it to anyone else. But I get up at half past four and I go out and put the coffee on and between about ten of five and about six thirty, every day, I write something. If I'm going to write a poem, that's good. If I'm not I practice. I try to—I take a truck or I take a telephone pole and I take a cat. I take something and I try to see if I can describe it....I'll tell you something, Bill, I used to get anxiety attacks at the idea of having to go out and throw bull to sell something to feed my family—until the idea occurred to me in this getting up early that, really, quite honestly I was doing what I wanted to do first every day before I had to go and do what I must for "the man"....

Q: *You do readings of your work from time to time. Do you find that you get anything as a creative artist from reading aloud your work or does it create any problems for you ?*

A: Well, it's a very difficult thing to answer. Number one, everybody has an ego and I'm certainly no different than anybody else. You work so long alone that the idea of being asked to read your work—if you're a human being—has to interest you. I suddenly find that the most important thing to me is if a professor will say to me later, somebody will say, "You know Leo, somebody heard you read your poems and they really want to look at one of your books"... now that means my work has reached someone I have never met and I think that Karl Shapiro gave me the finest definition of what a poem is: "A poem is an anonymous gift to an anonymous recipient"... and when you are finished with it, it doesn't belong to you anymore but to whoever wants it. So the value of poetry readings to me is if I can read my work and somewhere in that room somebody is touched enough or if somebody says, "I thought I was the only one who knew what it was to get your fingers cut while working in a soldering factory;" or—"I thought I was the only one who ever had that thought about the Staten Island Ferry."

Q: *I understand.*
A: And if I could do that then I feel that I'm in tune with the time I write in ...I'm talking too much and not saying much. Writers write, they don't talk!

Q: *You have also taught from time to time, poetry. Do you feel that helps or harms?*
A: Helps or harms who?

Q: *I'm talking about the process of your own writing. Does it help you to get in touch with your writing or does it take away from your writing?*
A: I think the value of writing workshops is that they create a job for the writer, for me; and for a lot of lonely, lonely people, they create an opportunity to come out of themselves and meet new people and make friendships. Most of the writers I know only teach at workshops because they have to eat.

Q: *Would you describe writing workshops as a social problem?*
A: Not social. They're like somebody coming to dinner to try to have you touch your forehead, as if in doing so you can say "Now go forth and be Edna St. Vincent Millay"....

Q: *You're describing it like a church.*

A: I'm describing it like an invention, an invention of lonely people to play at writing and an ingenious invention of real writers to work near their trade while they earn cash to pay their bills. Neat for all!

Q: *You never attended workshops yourself?*

A: No. I have gone to hear writers I respect hoping they could say something I could hear with my middle ear, with my inside gear and use. I've gone to the 92nd Street Y to hear a great writer read, or I've gone to hear a great writer lecture or read, but I have never signed up to take any workshop.

Q: *Do you feel that the workshops that you've taught, that the work has been on any level?*

A: I find that some writing students said I ought to go to hell and that they don't know why they paid to hear me and those people I have hope for—especially the ones who could tell me I know absolutely nothing. I'd think "could Thomas Wolfe have just left my class or Hart Crane or Delmore?"

Q: *We've talked earlier about solitude—which is the loneliness of a writer. Yes? Are there certain writers who have meant a lot to you, I mean, perhaps even been a reason you've written?*

A: Yes. But writing is such a singularly tough pursuit that you have to work at it and somebody doesn't eventually take you up, make moves for you, you can't have success. I've been very lucky. I've had you, Bill and thank you very much for all the space time after time in *The New York Quarterly*. I've had Karl Shapiro who, when I was young, took the time and this man had the Pulitzer Prize—he had everything and I was nobody; he took the time to write me and give me advice and to encourage me and I've had Richard Wilbur who is a gracious gentleman as well as a great, great writer when we need him most and I've had William Wallace Davidson, God rest his soul, who took my first poems at *The Georgia Review*, and I've had Richard Eberhart who to me is one of the most remarkable people, remarkable not only because he has genius, but he has the genius to touch and support all kinds of writing and to support it to support even the last thing he'd ever write....that blessed man!

Allen Ginsberg. Don't you kid yourself, Allen Ginsberg has one of the finest talents in America and has been most generous to other poets without ever letting anyone know about it. I think I've seen Allen Ginsberg maybe twice in my life. Probably at Saint Mark's Church and once in Washington Square Park walking around by the old hanging tree. Charles Bukowski, too, and Lynn Savitt....they're excellent and they're so good, like you are Bill, as to frighten the pompous and revitalize literature....I've found that real writers, the writers who write, are more than willing to try to do what they can for writing which really means you....Because helping you live, pay your rent, eat....in a way they're helping themselves....They're justifying themselves.... Their work really does that but since they are human beings, helping other writers does it better for their souls.

Q: *O.K. I'm going back to the beginning of this interview. I've asked you about the long poem. Poets have tried writing it and have fallen on their faces because they couldn't sustain a lyric impulse beyond two or three pages. You have recently been working on a trilogy of poems of which the first is* Coming to Cummington to Take Kelly. *And the second is* Shatterhouse. *You're working on the third part of the trilogy now. Is this something you propose to yourself? A huge structure like an architecture, and then you set yourself to complete it.*

A: When I was very young and drinking very heavily, and I could say that to you because I'm, well, we all think of what wasted our lives. And I was in Canada. Somebody asked Hemingway if Paris and London were wonderful cities to write in and he said they were wonderful cities but perhaps he wasn't so good when he was in them. Well, I think that I began to say to myself in my late twenties. "I'm going to do, as I live, the large trilogy of the condition of my country, its people, where we're at, or where we've been, where we may go. And before I can do it I'm going to practice. So I'm going to make the best short points I can. And then very slowly, I'm going to see if I can write a longer poem. But if there's a secret to the long narrative poem—You mentioned my book *Shatterhouse*. It's one poem, sixty-six pages long, in six parts. It either has something to say or it's going to fail. And if I don't have something to say and if it wasn't something that I felt was the culmination of everything I've ever been, or ever thought ever wanted to try to become, then it wouldn't have a chance of holding up. I think that some people who try long poems really have nothing at the center of the poem but wills.

Q: *I see.*
A: There is no simple idea. There is no intent. I feel that if you have a good intention, you've got to give it a race. You could come in twentieth just by intending to.

Q: *Yes.*
A: But if you have no intention you run 'im in the race. But either you drop out six miles down the road or you come in one thousandth.

Q: *When this interview is published, it will be common knowledge that you have received the Shelley Memorial Award from The Poetry Society of America. You have survived through your life as a salesman, as a teacher, at odd jobs. In one of your poems you even describe crossing America with a skillet that you kept clean as a way of insuring a day's job and some dining. Now you are coming into some recognition and awards. You must have gone through years of seeing other poets getting awards that you may have felt did not deserve them. How does this change in status make you feel?*
A: Let me answer you the only way I can: In the first place, no one ever asked me to write. And I am on my own. A writer is on his own or her own. I think that the help along the way and especially the acknowledgment by complete strangers that perhaps we put something valuable down, is very healthy. I think that I've come to feel this way about awards. It was, never will be a reason why I write or why any real writer writes, but on the other hand, it could get me a job. It could overcome things like a lack of sheepskin. Somebody could say, "We can have you now because so and so has given you this." I think other people's societies get pensions at the end of working years, and a lot of work is so alone and so all by himself; I think prizes let you know that someone, someone really did read and evaluate what you tried hard to write as no one else had written it. I think that does mean something. I don't think that

having a prize is either going to make you a writer or not make you a writer. I think what it may mean is: That a total stranger or a group of people that you may not have ever known existed, took the trouble to look at something that you tried to spend your life doing and said, "Well, gee, it looks like he tried good and well enough to get this" and what they give you might mean that you get a job. And I don't think that anyone who's sensible, who writes, really allows the possession of a prize in itself to influence them one way or another.

Q: *Let me ask you now, towards the end of this interview: Is there any question that you'd want to propose to yourself?*

A: I don't know where personal motivation is going to come from in America. I think I mean we're getting awfully good at heart transplants and computers; we're putting computers in front of children to talk to them and tell them how to multiply, how to do geometry, how to do everything for them. And I don't know, you know, a hungry man fights to get a meal, and I think that a good writer is hungry to write. I don't know what will motivate anyone in the future to try to write or to act or to put themselves into something. And I think that question is what I might be dealing with after I finish my trilogy. And I ask myself what will happen when I write for (free?) I mean, will I suddenly be ready to die?

Q: *You seem to have had very strong motivation throughout your life always to keep writing. Do you ever have any fear about that motivation dissipating?*

A: Well, many times. I, in fact, didn't get going until awfully late and who am I to think that I can write? I think any writer might say that you write because you can't help it.

Q: *You talked about motivation as a problem in our culture. Do you think that the proliferation of creative writing programs and the MFA degree have helped or hindered the motivation for writing really good poetry?*

A: I don't want to make people mad at me; but 1 will say this to you: I think that in order for the college process to succeed, if you turn someone over to a master of fine arts degree the next logical thing is: A job has to be found for them. And I think that perhaps the stress on that degree is stronger than on the ability and quality of the writing of the person who has that degree.

Q: *You keep talking about jobs, jobs, jobs. Does it occur to you that you would not perhaps have written the extraordinary poetry that you have written, if you had been a tenured English professor in some small college for forty years? But that because of the diversity of your experience that you draw from in your writing—*

A: I think that you're hitting on something that's very important. And I'm certainly not trying to correct you. I'd just like to bring something out: The reason I kept saying jobs, jobs, jobs. I have a wife, as you know, and a daughter. And I think that I made the decision to be responsible for my child and try to be responsible to contribute to my marriage and to our income. Now when I didn't have this feeling of responsibility, I wasn't being worried about a job. I didn't care where I was and I never thought about it. And if I was washing dishes in Seattle tonight and on a bus tomorrow or hitchhiking to Omaha, Nebraska tomorrow, I really didn't think about what would happen in Omaha. Suddenly, in my middle fifties, I'm wondering how I can educate my daughter or even how can I have an old age and if this job thing becomes an obsession. Because without one I don't know where I'll be. Or what will happen to me.

Q: *And yet the poetry still keeps getting written.*

A: Because it's all I want to do and it's all I've ever wanted to do, and I'm not very good at it. But, I certainly wasn't a novelist and I certainly was not a playwright. And I certainly wasn't an essayist. So the only thing left to me was to try to do this, and dammit I'm trying because 1 can't help myself.

Editor's note:
This essay is excerpted from Chapters 2 and 3 of Tim Peeler's MA thesis, *From the Wheel to the Moon: A Developmental Study of Leo Connellan's Poetry*, Appalachian State University, Boone, NC, 1992.

Unrealized Manhood in Leo Connellan's Poetry

Tim Peeler

Part I—"Lobster Claw"

"Lobster Claw" is the first of Connellan's early long poems, a poem that lends itself to a study of the poet's technique, as well as being a thematic seed for his later efforts. Given our late-twentieth-century tendency toward condensation and abbreviation, the first thing we note about "Lobster Claw" is the substantial length of the poem. Karl Shapiro calls Connellan "one of the few people who can hold up a long poem" (cover). More recently and romantically, Harry Brody suggests that the long poems "work because they are driven as far as they can go by a big red happy sad heart that has sentenced itself to the task of writing down a man in America in our holy, twisted time. Thus, his marrow narratives tell our story before it happens and, listenin' to him chink and hiss and cuss and crank way down where our ghosts are dust convinces us there's more in the crimes our hearts confess" (letter, 29 August, 1991). The reader is drawn forward in the poem by a sense of emotional momentum, for Connellan truly has a "voice that sustains through shifting emotions, a voice that speaks as if the gun were always to the head and the truth were the only way out" (Calhoun 24).

But "Lobster Claw" and the other long poems succeed because of the writer's consistent ability to sustain not only the emotional but also the technical aspects of the work. Although the elements of poetry (lyrical sense, metaphor, alliteration, rhythm) are central, there is a willingness on the part of the poet to allow a fictional structure to frame the work on a more concrete base. Characters are introduced, become involved in conflict and usually reach some type of resolution. These fictive elements may not always be obvious, but they nevertheless help guide the reader like the "deep structure" in a novel.

As is the case in most of the early work, "Lobster Claw" is written in a spare, tight framework characterized by brief but rhythmic lines, creating what Richard Wilbur calls "a wiriness in the movement" (cover). The narrative is direct, the tone harsh, and the oddly broken lines quick as a boxer's jab. Enriched meaning is the result of this structure, because, in lacking adornment, it simulates the life depicted in the lines.

The speaker is an old lobsterman who begins his story with this chilling statement in the opening two-line verse: "Morning and I / must kill" (*New and Collected Poems* 171). We read this as one line. Immediately the reader is introduced to a line break technique that the poet uses constantly to enrich the meaning of his work. But by grouping the first three words, Connellan also hints at the relationship between the narrator and the morning. This is a man who has risen early for countless years to undertake his labor on the sea. Morning is the dance partner in his daily survival, the co-conspirator. With this introduction, the poet opens the door to a world where the polar opposites of the life cycle intermingle, where contrasting elements like great hope and utter disappointment coexist.

The second stanza introduces the theme of isolation. The lobsterman rises to the loneliness of "one-bulb light crashing/ black dying night to/ cowardly dawn" (161). The image of the "one-bulb light" is the key to this stanza. Connellan chose this image to help the reader actually see the early morning struggle of the narrator in his dimly lit house. The one-bulb light represents the lobsterman's "vicious niche" in this world. The lobsterman is isolated in the quiet dark of the morning and by the pure necessity of what he must do.

And within this isolation the lobsterman questions the morality of his trade, identifying himself with "all murderers" and revealing the kind of fear that accompanies fatigue, "a twig snap jolts me" (171). In the remaining five stanzas of Part One, the narrator addresses the lobster in a tone that indicates an affection for its spirit, yet a stoic resignation toward the day's work. The respect is similar to that of the native

Americans for their prey, but the lobsterman stops short of apology:

> ...I will kill you now,
> crouch in your rocks. Pull up
> your bed covers of seaweed.
> Ride the sea's bottom. Move
> out deep in winter. Burrow
> in mud ...
> I will bait you
> to my family's survival
> without conscience. (171)

But he wants this activity to be a worthy one and is willing to rationalize: "God/ you must want me to/ do this. Perhaps/ the ocean with all its/ bluff is not big enough/ to keep all you lobster" (172). The use of "God" in this passage is another important stroke in the poet's technical strategy for the poem. It can be read either as the narrator addressing his religious "God," or as despairing slang spoken directly to the lobster. The rationalization echoes that of most abusers, seeking a sense of self-forgiveness in denial. The dubious attitude toward lobstering as asserted by the poet through his narrator may again mirror Connellan's complex attitude toward his home state. The first part concludes with the narrator resolving to lay out a string of traps that the lobster can't resist.

Already in the first part of "Lobster Claw" there are instances of word combinations and usages that distinguish Connellan's work throughout his career. The use of functional shift is pervasive in the early work and is also peppered throughout *The Clear Blue Lobster-Water Country*. While a reviewer praises this technique, "His inversions, alliterations and use of nouns as adjectives give some of his lines the toughness of Beowo1f" (Robb 4C), a reader might wonder about overuse. Such concern may be a momentary reaction, as Harry Calhoun suggests: "Connellan has a genius for inserting a seemingly inappropriate word into a line so that it jars the reader, shatters and reforms his/her expectations—and then, when the reader reflects, the word choice seems perfect" (23). Hayden Carruth asserts that Connellan's "oddly original" phrasings give his work "the quality of the permanently new" (8C). Connellan unglues the language and pieces it back together in his own way.

Part Two of "Lobster Claw" introduces the ideological conflict between the oldtime lobstermen and the "Youngsters" who "no longer work the long hours" (172). The actual conflict is between the new technology of industrial fishing and the oldtimer's intuition and finesse. Airplanes and scuba divers have eliminated the need for men like the oldtimer. There is no outwitting the trap and winning the bait. In Part Three the oldtimer declares, "It is over, men like me? out in boats in the/ great sea days" (173). His vision of "men like me" is tainted by a substantial amount of romantic embroidery. As in a frontier folktale, he remembers his compatriots:

> ... a breed of men
> who could keep such
> generated strength in our
> sinews and wills as to
> break the back of a bear
> on a handful of food a
> day and walk a hundred
> miles. (173)

As in later work, particularly the trilogy, this struggle between idealism and new technology is not totally a protest against technology. Rather, Connellan contends that certain attitudes have developed as the American lifestyle has softened. He perceives the existence of this attitude as a society-wide problem that invades even his own craft, where the new generation is not "willing to submit [their work] and take abuse" (letter). Both the artist and the lobsterman seem to be philosophically isolated at this point.

Another central character is introduced in the second part of this poem, that of the personified "sea mother." Here the sea is represented as a kind of nature god:

> ... a womb, frothy
> like blushing lovers are
> shy, but within her,
> after all, are the lives
> of her many children
> killing among themselves. (172)

In this portrayal of the sea as a microcosm of life, the poet/narrator again focuses on our tendency toward murderousness. The sea is noted for her harshness: "she strikes down hard/ those too naive to learn/ that she is a sea not to be taken" (172). The lobsterman asserts that he is "not easily caught" (172), his declaration reemphasizing the state of the abuser as victim. He doesn't directly address the sea mother again till the final part of the poem, but her subtle presence is definite throughout the work. And he never forgets that his daily purpose is to "rip out her children" (180). (Connellan's traditional choice of the sea/mother analogy is an interesting one. In the later work, and in his own life, the mother is often depicted as a calming force, the influence that stifles the murderer in all of us.)

Parts Four and Five follow the lives of the lobstermen off the violent ocean and into the desperation and violence of their existence on land. The narrator exclaims that "Saturday night is/ always our time" (174). But the despair of living in "thin frame houses" with "pinched women" (174) is made worse by his vision of the future when:

> ... our sons
> will be out on the
> boats with us soon, our
> girls rushed to
> the first men who
> will support them,
> whether there is love. (174)

The lobsterman knows all too well that he is locked into this frightening cycle. He knows that the weekend drinking and fights are an inevitable part of it "the getting the seal and futility of you Saturday night" (175). Among the townspeople there is ignorance, prejudice toward outsiders, and as seen in Part Five, a way of life not unlike that within the sea where the "many children" kill "among themselves" (172).

In Part Five Connellan provides a contrast to the deeply ingrained lobstertown experience. The "postmaster's son," like the poet, has escaped the "wind-burned" life. He again proves his "kind of brains" by avoiding a fight and then leaving the Saturday night dance most appropriately, before drink and despair drive one of the envious lobstermen to send him "home in a basket of aggravation" (176). This contrast is significant because it voices the most prominent theme in Connellan's work: control.

Viewing this substantial mass of emotionally-charged poetry, veering through its tight twists and unexpected bends, stumbling sometimes on its awkwardness, the reader must finally realize that *control* is at the core of its vision. Beyond style, beyond technique, the poet wants us to focus on the lobsterman's inability to direct his own life. He has given up on options, so much so that he even foresees the doom of his children. He has abdicated his right to choose consciously. Like the other "anguished figures in Connellan's tragic poems," he has been "shaped by life, has allowed things to happen to him, has been passive, and has become rather than made himself" (Calhoun 2). The feelings of the lobsterman, who exists in this trap of self-doubt and despair, could easily be summed up by the last lines of another poem , "Mundelein on the Michigan": "...it is not my life, I am the / wolf with the lamb in his teeth, / why did God turn me around?" (166) In the poet's estimation, the lobsterman, through his loss of conscious choice, has become less than a man should be.

Part II—"When Did My Manhood Wake!"

To discern the origin of Connellan's concept of unrealized manhood, we must turn again to the poet's ever-revealing personal experience. According to Connellan, he was raised during a less child-oriented time period in our history (1930s) when a child was expected to be seen and not heard. Parents were simply not as open with their children about sexuality or feelings in general (Connellan interview). He has often described himself as "one of the last published poets raised without the benefit of psychiatry" (1). He further contends that psychiatry "evolved out of the Second World War. Before, most people did not realize that we all have individual and true emotions that can be disturbed by influences, by being indoctrinated by people we come to love, so that if we do not behave just the way Dad wants us to, we will lose his love.... Psychiatry was not really accepted in the United States until Mom and Sister and Wife had just two choices: they could accept psychiatry or call their sons, brothers, and husbands cowards because they couldn't stand the sound of bombs and explosions in war, and they froze up" (6).

Connellan refers to his adolescence as "late adolescence," one experienced between the age of twenty and thirty rather than in the early teens. In his estimation, this was not just a matter of immaturity, but instead a rational reaction to his being sent into an unforgiving world without the necessary knowledge to cope. He strongly believes that he represents a generation of men and women raised in this manner, and that delayed or prolonged adolescence was the common result.

"When did my manhood wake to its dying!" (184) is the tortured exclamation that begins the short but powerful poem "Watching Jim Shoulders." This first-person account contrasts the degree to which individuals have asserted control over their lives. For the poet, it is a statement of self-realization. In the midst of his heavy drinking days, Connellan had chosen to remain sober and attend a Colorado rodeo. He was fortunate enough to see the legendary cowboy Jim Shoulders and was so impressed that he wrote the poem on the spot (Connellan interview). The incredible ability and determination of Shoulders awakened in him the fear of losing control over his own life choices. Getting this exemplary glimpse at human potential, Connellan found himself wanting.

Although visually different from "Lobster Claw," "Watching Jim Shoulders" shares some technical characteristics. The poem is, of course, shorter and the lines are longer, but they are still oddly if not randomly broken, as if the line breaks had been left up to the words. The language is still spare, simple, and straightforward. Again there is attention to repetitive sound in phrases like "sophistication is silence," and "wrist flicked instantly" (184). Although technique enriches meaning here, it seems less important, and oddly broken lines are possibly just the result of spontaneity. "Watching Jim Shoulders" is a poem that asks to be examined for content rather than its concrete structure.

In doing so, we must first look at the contrasting characters (narrator/rodeo cowboy). What is so different about their approaches to living, and why is the effect on the narrator so profound? "Inside," the final word in line 2, is the key to understanding the difference the poet has ascertained between himself and Jim Shoulders. "Inside" is where the troublesome path of Connellan's life has led. This "inside" is not just "New England or Elko, Nevada." "Inside," rather, is another name for Connellan's symbolic trap. The first three lines of "Watching Jim Shoulders" are a lament for time wasted "inside." One has to emerge from the trap to gain some understanding of personal shortcomings. In "Lobster Claw" the lobsterman accepted his life in the trap because he had no other frame of reference. He had no Jim Shoulders, but Connellan, during his travels, perceives Shoulders working his cowboy magic in the "vast wide-open space," in the "remote private/ America of ranges" (184). The shocking contrast between Jim Shoulders' world and the narrator's is so tremendous that the poet must introduce it with a sense of reverence. He does so with this religious metaphor: "air and snow like first communion lace on/ "blunt mountains." creating a moral juxtaposition between whorehouses, "inside screen doors with legal girls," and "communion lace" (184).

In this "outside" world, the narrator encounters sophistication and truth in the simple states of silence and calculated physical action. The life-conquering Jim Shoulders is the mirror that he cannot turn away from. Connellan carries the scars of his own agonizing past, but he notes that Shoulders is "Mantle on horseback..." although he is "as injured" (184). Even the coincidence of the cowboy's name reminds one of strength, responsibility, and control. The poet builds on the theme of control with this metaphor of Shoulders in action:

> scraping the cheeks of steers along earth cut by
> grooves of his boot heels, while those horns that could
> cave in ribs, turned until the folds in the animal's
> neck looked like its spine would split through skin,
> yet didn't in this master's hands. (184)

Jim Shoulders is but one of Connellan's manhood heroes, for the concept of unrealized, threatened, or distorted manhood is central to his work. It usually revolves around the theme of personal control and manifests itself in character after character. In the early work it is so pervasive that, as Calhoun points out, "Connellan seems to be writing the same poem over and over, finding the same things to grapple with in hundreds of dissimilar situations" (letter).

Part III—"They smashed the Butterfly/ against a wall"

In order to discuss and develop examples of unrealized manhood, Connellan had first to establish for himself a firm concept of ideal manhood. In doing so, he could not rely on the cultural perceptions often embodied in popular film and literature of his time. What is revealed in his work is a seemingly unattainable idealistic entity. For Connellan, a "real man" does not simply exert physical prowess over those in his charge. Although the "manhood hero" may possess physical prowess, like Jim Shoulders, internal control is much more important. It therefore becomes possible for his heroes to differ as vastly as rodeo cowboy Jim Shoulders, or baseball player Mickey Mantle, or Spanish poet Federico Garcia Lorca. In this work, manhood is not obtained overnight or in a stylized coming-of-age quest. Rather, it is a manner of living that develops through maturity and understanding. It occurs over time as one learns better to make conscious choices. Harry Calhoun relates this concept well:

> To me, Connellan's concept [of manhood] is similar to the ancient Roman idea of the *vir*. It was important to Roman men that they be *viri*, that is, men who embodied the virtues of courage, learning, and a certain gentlemanliness. (We get our word "virile" from this root.) To this idea Connellan adds the elements of brotherly love and, importantly, the idea of conscious choice. (letter)

In Connellan's emotionally charged "Lament For Federico Garcia Lorca," the element of brotherly love is sorely lacking. In trying to gain an understanding of the murder of Lorca, the poet creates a scathing indictment of a segment of humanity for what he perceives as a cruelty that is an inherent part of our nature. The essential truth, according to Connellan, is that Lorca was killed because his murderers were not men. By using the pronoun "we," Connellan acknowledges the existence of his own murderous tendencies and repeats this refrain later as if to remind himself: "Yes, I know we are only children, / children picking up the smatterings / of what we can." (66)

This poem focuses on very specific reasons for unrealized manhood, such as immaturity, insecurity, and the inability to act independently.

These reasons, combined with intolerance, give birth to that insensitive group, capable of smashing "the Butterfly/ against a wall" (65). Insecurity is not new here. This was one of the same qualities acted upon by the lobstermen at their Saturday night dance. In "Lobster Claw," insecurity helps fuel "the blood of good fights" (174).

In "Lament" insecurity is shown to be a strong obstacle to Connellan's concept of manhood:

> the boys among us
> will grow up and marry the girls
> trying endlessly to prove our manhood.
>
> Some of us never can.
> We will always think it is in question,
> that all eyes focus on us as un-men.
> We will murder anyone
> who does not feel a need to prove it. (65)

When the narrator asserts that Lorca was "killed because he/ wore skirts in the heart of his trousers" (65), he is not simplifying the murder into a form of "gay bashing." It becomes rather a symbol for all killings that occur as a result of insecurity or the lack of brotherly love.

Again at the heart of Connellan's explanation is the lack of control that exists in the mob that killed Lorca. In conversation Connellan admits to the existence of this dark possibility in his own makeup. Interestingly, he describes himself as one being composed of three persons. First there is Leo Connellan, the poet, writer, teacher, lecturer. Then there is Leo, the survivor, who must (to borrow from Eliot) maintain a face for the faces he meets. This Leo has sold stationery, flipped burgers, and swept hallways. Finally, there is the potential killer, the conscienceless, ambitious cold one (phone conversation). But Connellan doesn't drag people out of their houses at sunrise. He maintains control, as we all must, over that part of himself. More horrible to him than the fact that Lorca was "deprived of one more sun/ before forever dark" (66), is the knowledge that "We will let it happen again," because "we are children" (66), not fully men, who will not take control of the next situation.

The dark tone of this poem is generated by the horror both alluded to and graphically depicted. This is the type of poem referred to by Hayden Carruth as a "tough poem, by no means calculated to cheer anyone up, but in its honesty and urgency, effective" (8C). Honesty is the key concept for understanding the purpose of the violence in Connellan's poetry. He wishes to depict this tragic reality as it stunningly but truly exists. That is the spirit with which he delivers descriptions of children who pluck the eyes out of kittens, and, even more cruelly:

> tie Cats' tails together and
> toss them over a clothesline
> feeling warm pleasure
> witnessing their frantic clawing
> each other to death. (65)

The violence in Connellan's work is not gratuitous. He intends for it to convey meaning, and in the case of "Lament," to involve the reader emotionally to the point where he/she can feel the "shame" in which "the capes of Spain/ folded themselves" (66). He wants to expose the idealistic myth of childhood innocence. In doing so he insists that we spotlight the kinds of childhood incidents that have been unconsciously removed to the far reaches of memory. Connellan seems to say that if we look and admit that we did this in childhood and that this is why we are still intolerant and murderous, then maybe we can change. On the surface this is not a poem of hope. But beyond the poet's insistence that we will murder again, there must be a greater reason for talking to "children/ who will do it again" (66). There must be some glimmer of hope.

The style and structure of "Lament" are typical of the early poems. It is composed with the taut wiriness of "Lobster Claw," often with only three words to a line. Occasionally a line will run long, with as many as ten syllables, seemingly at random. But upon closer examination, this occurs each time in order to focus on an important image, like "children picking up the smatterings," and the poem begins to read like varying angles of a camera lens.

Connellan applies his customarily simple diction, which accentuates some of the more striking word choices. The most pronounced is his use of "smatterings" in line 6 and repeated in line 42. The image of gathering broken, scattered things is effective. "Smatterings," like the paint dripped from the artist's brush, come to us in a second-hand manner. This image signals a vague chaos, symbolic of the uncontrolled life of these "un-men." The word "smatterings" even sounds like a comparatively diminishing phrase, "small matters."

The oddest phrase in this poem occurs in the first line: "In the early dawn bleak cold" (65). Connellan alters the emphasis in this phrase by relegating the adjectives "bleak" and "cold" to the end of the line. The effect of these words would have lessened if they had been placed in the expected slot between "the" and "early." By changing the syntax, Connellan immediately focuses on words that will affect the tone of the poem. Lorca is executed in the bleakness before sunrise. And the outlook for his coldhearted killers, and hence humanity, is also bleak. The cynical if not darkly pessimistic attitude of the speaker flows from this opening line. That phrasing in line one is a primary example of Connellan's ability to make the language work uniquely for him. The phrase is itself an appeal for the reader to suspend normal syntactical expectations and to experience a radical vitality in the language.

Such radical vitality, in language and in content, brings to life the tensions between manhood and control at the core of Connellan's vision. In portraying a lobsterman, a rodeo cowboy, and a Spanish poet, Connellan's self-portrait, humane and compassionate, emerges and remains with readers.

WORKS CITED

Calhoun, Harry. Review of *The Clear Blue Lobster-Water-Country*, by Leo Connellan. *Third Lung Review* 1989: 23-24.

—— "The First Pitch." *Third Lung Review*, 1991: 2-7.

—— Letter to the Author. 21 June, 1990.

Carruth, Hayden. Review of *First Selected Poems*, by Leo Connellan. *New York Times Book Review* 23 May, 1976: 8C.

Connellan, Leo. *The Clear Blue Lobster-Water Country*. New York: Harcourt Brace Jovanovich, 1985.

—— *New and Collected Poems*. New York: Paragon House. 1989.

—— *First Selected Poems*. University of Pittsburgh Press, 1976.

—— Letter to the Author. 28 July, 1988.

—— Telephone Interview. 8 October, 1988.

—— Telephone Interview. 27 October, 1988.

—— Telephone Interview. 10 August, 1991.

Robb, Christina. “Sea is a Womb.....” Review of First Selected Poems, by Leo Connellan. *Boston Globe* July, 1976: 4C

Shapiro, Karl. Back cover quote from *First Selected Poems*, by Leo Connellan. Pittsburgh: University of Pittsburgh Press, 1976.

Warren, Robert Penn. Back cover quote from *First Selected Poems*, by Leo Connellan. Pittsburgh: University of Pittsburgh Press, 1976.

Wilbur, Richard. Back cover quote from *First Selected Poems*, by Leo Connellan. Pittsburgh: University of Pittsburgh Press, 1976.

from *The Maine Poems* by Leo Connellan, 1999

FOREWORD TO *THE MAINE POEMS*

Sanford Phippen

Leo Connellan of Rockland, Maine is a great and important poet; and Maine people should know about him and read his work because much of what is permanent in the soul of Maine is preserved in his poetry.

When I first read Connellan, twenty years ago, I recognized right away the lost world of my own coastal Maine. Here was a soulmate, a brother, and a powerful poet who grew up in working class Downeast the same way I did. Even though I grew up in the Ellsworth-Mount Desert Island area, the life of the people—my own people—was essentially the same as that of the Rockland fishermen, sardine packers, waitresses, and truck drivers that people the poems of Leo Connellan. His poetry excites me, not just because of the truth-telling and the easy identification, but because of the way in which he writes: he's a convivial and garrulous Maine man with a sharp eye and a great sense of humor, swapping jokes and stories with a bunch of pals in a bar, or down on the dock, telling it like it really is with no holds barred, no censorship, no glossing over. But at the same time, his is the voice of the poet who is a master of the tongue. I love Leo's words, the way he expresses himself. He makes me think of my father, uncles, other Maine men who have suddenly found a brilliant way to articulate their innermost thoughts and deepest feelings.

In 1983, the Humanities Division of the University of Tampa published *Festschrift*, a symposium in book form, compiled in honor of Connellan upon the occasion of the poet's having won the Shelley Memorial Award. Twenty-three poets and writers, including such well-known ones as Richard Eberhart, William Stafford, Hayden Carruth, and Donald Junkins, were contributors to this volume.

Maine native poet Kendall Merriam, who grew up in Rockland as did Connellan, offered a "Poem for Leo," in which he says:

Rockland is an anti-intellectual town
if you don't play football
or haul lobsters you have to leave...

a town that doesn't love
pimply faced, gangling boys who write po'try
the town that drives them all away
all of my friends are out-of-staters now
Leo is an out-of-stater now
a Maine boy who made good
with no help from Maine
except for the pain he suffered here
he is a great poet no thanks to Rockland...

But in part, the greatness of Connellan's Maine poems is indeed thanks to Rockland and the poet's lifelong quarrel with his hometown; Rockland, or "Lime City," as he calls it in his work, provides the haunting subject matter, the bittersweet memories, and the creative rage that enriches his best poems.

As Connellan himself says in his poem "Wawenock":

It is my night for tears.
Pine tree, umbrella for blueberries,
I am gone, forever from Lime City,
vanished as though an Indian never
slid across Chicawaukee Lake
like all night on a match flame...

In "Sea Gulls Wait," he writes:

Come sea gulls, come! I am weak now
In this instant of home, like walking
the earth after my time, the town never
loved me, but I have an ache for this place,
forever the pain is there...

Throughout his Maine poems there is the theme of loss: the loss of his mother, who died when he was seven; the loss of family and friends; the loss of home; and the loss of Maine, which he left at 19.

In his Foreword to *Death in Lobsterland* (1978), novelist Hubert Selby, Jr. writes: "These poems come from that part of the soul that's eternally longing to come home, no matter what we may believe is waiting for us. There is that insatiable hunger within all of us to know more than we know, to know the secret of leaves and rocks, to know our mother and father, to know ourselves. And we try to know ourselves by looking around us, but this only tells WHERE we are, not WHO we are. These poems are a song to the WHO we are all looking for through the confusion of our own lobsterland."

In 1995, Sue Walker, editor of *Negative Capability* at the University of Alabama, issued another Festschrift on Connellan, as part of the magazine, which featured eighteen of Connellan's poems as well as tributes from both Leo's wife Nancy and daughter Amy.

Survival in the Maine of the 1930s and '40s into which Connellan was born and raised depended upon killing: fishing the coastal waters, chopping down the trees, and hunting deer, birds, and other wildlife for food. Life was hard and basic with the majority of people employed in fish factories, saw mills, lumber and paper mills, on thin-soiled farms, on the railroads and boats, wherever they could find work. Rockland was a working man's town; and Connellan writes wonderfully and movingly about survival among the working folk he knew well.

At the opening of his poem "Lobster Claw," he writes:

> Lobster, I will kill you now,
> crouch in your rocks. Pull up
> your bed covers of seaweed.
> Ride the sea's bottom. Move
> out deep in winter. Burrow
> in mud. Hide under
> kelp. I will bait you
> to my family's survival
> without conscience. My own
> life is in the lines hauling you in. ..

And in his long poem "Amelia, Mrs. Brooks of My Old childhood," he writes:

Great lady of Sardines and
earth and blood, of
blueberryin' years, Clam Factory
years who brought up
children without help, a hopeless
drunk husband beating you in
his futility, when the country was smashed. ..

In "By the Blue Sea," another long, unforgettable poem, Connellan writes about a fisherman whose clothes "always smelled of gasoline and fish" and of his "Fish Woman," who suffers from lifelong unrequited love and from being married to a "mean and furious husband." Fish Woman finally leaves her husband and five boys to go and live a completely different life in Boston.

To survive in Connellan's Maine one needed a good sense of humor; and Connellan is deeply, truthfully funny the way Tennessee Williams' tragedies are funny, the way Thomas Wolfe's novels are funny, the way Flannery O'Connor's stories are funny, the way Mark Twain is funny.

Another of Connellan's themes is escape the way he escaped from Rockland and Maine; but he also writes about the people who can't or won't escape. In the poem "In Lobster Night," he writes about the local guy who works on a boat, hangs around a bar called "The Passion Pit," gets drunk, has sex with girls in his car. It begins:

Otto Fishinfolk, he's
everywhere you go.

Home, just off train,
to the house for a quick change

and that joy of first rushing
downtown to see Main Street again.

Otto's there. "In N'York, aincha!"
"Yes, I am." "Like hit? "I miss

home." "Ayuh, I know hit!"
"Well, see you Otto."

But no, "Hey now, you cummin'
with me tonight. We goin' t'git laid."

There's a poem titled "Maine," in which he writes about how "...Maine cannot provide for its bright youth," and which concludes:

...There are potatoes here, big as beach balls!
Fish, Lobster, Clams, Sardines. If you're from Maine
your heart is here but nothing for you.

Among some of the Maine native people who appear in Connellan's poetry runs a thread of mean spiritedness that is learned and a product from over the generations of the bitter, hardscrabble existence that too many Mainers have had to endure from the end of the so-called glorious ship-building days of the 19th century through the Depression years of the 1930s and well into recent times. An ugly bitter residue remains; and it's evident in the way neighbors and relatives won't help others out. People in small towns can be anything but nice to one another, snickering over someone's failure or shortcoming. These types of people don't do anything themselves, but if someone does manage to do something, they want that person to fail so they can laugh at him or her behind their back.

Richard Eberhart has said of Connellan's work: "He writes from an honesty and force which grapple with the pain of living and the drug of dreams; his work is harsh, direct, truth-telling .... he gives us long poems informed with dark colors, with tragic awareness." Poet Karl Shapiro has written: "The narrative strength reminds me of Robinson Jeffers, the other American ocean poet: "There is nothing stagy about the anguish and nothing fake about the force of the lines." And poet Thomas McGrath has said, "Leo Connellan's poems are not for lovers of the genteel, indeed, it would be difficult to find a poet who seems more ferociously intent on forcing upon us the hard news of failure, the failure of age, of the innocence of youthful hope—even (God help us) the failure of that perennial failure, the American dream. There are many fine short poems and they balance out the longer ones, and it is in the longer poems that Connellan shows his greatest power."

Whether Leo is writing about picking blueberries, the ravages of alcoholism, or about being an Irish Catholic in Protestantland, his poetry is full of great energy and life-giving spirit and rich with earthiness and honest passion. He is often raw, harsh, angry, and profane; but so is life. However, there are marvelous whoops to be had amongst the tragedy, pain, and sadness.

William Packard, the former editor of *The New York Quarterly*, which published a number of Connellan poems, wrote the most comprehensive and lengthy appreciation of Connellan in the 1983 *Festschrift*. About Leo the man, he says: "...I remember he always gestured a lot with his hands and he had a voice that would go from soft conspiracy whisper to laughing raucous laughter to a crooning lyric lilt as he read his latest poems out loud. I remember he always had such a strong sense of terror in the air, was always in some turmoil, would always be talking about which people were out to get him and what godawful things were about to happen, and then he would suddenly switch off into an ironic HAR DE HAR HAR voice of some seedy con pitchman. ..I wasn't always sure what to make of this powerhouse poet who was such a walking anthology of voices yet through all the voices there was that Yankee nasal Maine twang that betrayed his own origins, and behind all the paranoia fits and all the verbal hyperventilations, real or imagined, any fool could plainly see that Leo Connellan was a great large heart that would not be denied, and anyone who read over his poems could see that here was an enormous talent that was hellbent on finding its form and taking final shape."

In a review of Connellan's *Shatterhouse*, the second book of his acclaimed trilogy *The Clear Blue Lobster-Water Country* (1985), Packard writes about Connellan the poet, comparing him to Allen Ginsberg, Hart Crane, John Steinbeck, and Eugene O'Neill. As Packard says, "*Shatterhouse* is an ode to America, to American literature, to the damned madness of American families, to the quackery of American psychiatric practices, to the eccentricities of American sexuality, to the American bloodstream violence that is all around us always, and it is also an ode to the human mind and to its ability to cure itself of its own worst illnesses. With the writing of *Shatterhouse*, Leo Connellan assumes his place as major poet in America today, probably better, and from now on we'll have to look backward for comparisons, to all those poets and prose writers Connellan was always reminding us of—Walt Whitman and Stephen Crane and Federico Garcia Lorca and Hart Crane and Washington Irving."

In the 1985 spring issue of *The Greenfield Review*, poet Donald Junkins writes of Connellan and Rockland: "At the heart of Leo Connellan's poems is the sea gull's diet, a documentary spirit, and a lyrical narrative voice. No one writes as well about Maine, its coastal punishments and its inland Spartan ways. Downeast life is the material substance of Connellan's poems, and in them the lobster and its industry becomes his double-edged and ironic metaphor, from *Death in Lobsterland* (1978) to the... rare trilogy, *The Clear Blue Lobster-Water Country* (1985). Connellan's subjects are daily life in Maine: its herring industry ("a seine around fish in moon black"); its neighbor-deaths ("cuddling his shoulder with the check of a healed broken neck"); its earth rottings ("the long sealed tight lips of the town code"); and its agonizing blood ocean ("granite and lime country, lobster, plush berries popping the hills, Maine my Maine of wild rhubarb, sweet spruce and pine trees, dandelion greens pulled fresh out of your front lawns"). Out of his boyhood life in Rockland, Connellan remembers himself into his Maine poems, and his subjects weigh their biographical anchors under the gull metaphors that transcend history and narrative and remembered denial...The lobster is both the red and the black in Connellan's verse and no one understands its shifty mobilities better. The jewel of the sea-mine; the lucre of lost causes."

In the 1990s, Connellan has returned to Maine almost every year to read and talk at the University of Maine in Orono, Bowdoin College, Bates College, the University of Maine at Farmington, College of the Atlantic, and a number of high schools including Orono, Houlton, and Ellsworth.

At Orono Public Library, teacher and poet Alex McLean introduced Leo once by saying: "With vivid, burnished words he has documented his 'impossibly rare' life. Like Frost, he has had a 'lover's quarrel' with his world, and his life and work are tidal in their coming and going...Wallace Stegner once wrote that 'a place is not a place until someone has written a poem about it.' Because of Leo's ardent investment, Rockland is indeed a place, and Maine is more of a place, and the hard green earth is more of a place. His eye focuses on the primary colors and the primary emotions. You won't find mauve, fuchsia, or magenta in these poems; rather, you will be washed in the blue of the sea, the green of the forest, and in a thousand shades of gray."

In 1996, Leo Connellan became the Poet Laureate of Connecticut and in May 1998 at graduation at the University of Maine at Augusta he was awarded an Honorary Doctorate degree.

Poet Constance Hunting, Professor of English at the University of Maine, who has invited Leo to her poetry classes several times and published him in her literary magazine *Puckerbrush Review,* once told me: "One time I was driving through Dover-Foxcroft at early evening and I saw this fireball going through this farmyard and I thought, 'That's Leo!'"

Connellan's latest book, *Short Poems, City Poems*, 1944-1998 (1998), carries a back cover quote from poet Robert Creeley, who lives in Waldoboro and who has recently been awarded the Bollingen Prize from Yale. Mr. Creeley writes: "Leo Connellan's integrity has been a measure for his fellow poets for years and years now...his perception and care are as ever unique—his heart a persistent refuge for anyone of us, in any time, in any place." Such a quote from Creeley conveys an example of the universal high regard that American poets have for Connellan's work.

Speaking for himself, Dr. Leo "fireball" Connellan has written: "Since you insist, I'll say this as some statement about the act of creating. I think the trick of writing is simplicity. The thing to do is to edit. Once the idea is clear, get rid of excess words. Excess words reveal the writer is bluffing behind nothing to say. I don't rush. The poem will be done when it is. But the minute you have to explain it you're writing prose. Since I often attempt long poems, I hope that I can count on argument with one's self giving my work a chance of being poetry, rather than rhetoric. There are two ways we write. Either we are born brilliant or something disturbs us. All good writing is realized by us because of what the writer has written for the reader to fill in." What the reader fills in with Connellan is truth.

from *The Ellsworth American*, "Spotlight," February 13-19, 1992

Young Poet Continues the Bardic Tradition

Sanford Phippen

In August 1990, Keith Therrien, who had just finished his junior year at the University of Maine and was working as a waiter in Bar Harbor, happened to go to a poetry reading by a well-known poet and Portland native Leo Connellan, at Monteux Hall in Hancock.

It was an evening that changed not only the way young Keith Therrien looked at the world, but the way in which he wrote his own poetry.

Hearing Connellan read helped Therrien find his own voice. As an English major with a concentration in creative writing, Keith was preparing for a life as an English teacher and poet; but that night he found out, among other things, that Leo Connellan had worked most of his life not as a teacher but as a salesman.

Therrien was familiar with Connellan's acclaimed trilogy *The Clear Blue Lobster-Water Country* when he composed the following poem:

Poet as Shoe Salesman

Oh, Leo Connellan, of the red-faded thin-napped carpet shoe
store country, where are your words? Why won't anyone
listen to your stories of deceit and pride and of the
time your grandfather came home to his granite house
that he built with his own hands and looked at you,
spit in his whiskers, blood in his eyes and said shut up!
I don't want to hear it anymore and the clock in the hall
started to gong in time with the crashing waves that
washed the priest's body ashore next to the barges
of the baked bean factory and all your father said
to your mother was shut up!—and life was brutal

for an Irish immigrant.
In the red-faded thin-napped carpet shoe store country
in the dangerous depression that comes with faded dreams'
false securities that quickly give way to living as an
artist groveling with the phone company, fumbling
with a green plastic shoe horn embossed with the golden
words Hush Puppies bringing new meaning to censorship
—the day St. Dominic's on Congress Street burned and
left the east side without religion or the time the
dolphin got caught in the tide down at the flats and
we hung it on a tree—285 pounds of dead inverted
fish meat—are fodder for pages and pages in the
red-faded thin-napped carpet shoe store country.
In the red-faded thin-napped carpet shoe store country
the boots jump down from their shelves and march across
your resolve and stamp out the secret code of your life
—time catching up, history slowly gaining on you
until it's right there over your shoulder sweating
and then passing you like a well conditioned marathon
runner making you feel old and dead but the ocean is
still breathing and the lobsters are still clawing
at their nets and the light that made bright the pages
that you were reading burned out so get up and get
on the road and sell your wares—sell yourself.
Come on, lady, buy the pumps. He needs the commission.

No matter that St. Dominic's Church isn't on Congress Street in Portland, the poem was accepted for publication by Constance Hunting (Keith's writing teacher at the University of Maine) for her literary magazine *Puckerbrush Review* along with another poem "A Perfect Place for Clams," and they both appeared in the summer 1991 issue.

A Perfect Place for Clams

There was a path leading from the steps of Easterly One
down to the shore lined with old rotting pots put
there as someone's idea of quaint New Englandness
while up the road Dwight, who keeps his metal traps

piled neatly in the back yard pissed because they're
not in the water where they could do him the most
good, never concerns himself with quaint.
The path opens up onto a cropping of rock, sea-split and
grainy from whipping sand and curves around and down
to the beach made out of weather crushed snail shells
and the seagull carcass rots in its coat of seaweed
and bluebottles while a man of war with its tentacles
all pulled under and looking like a four week old jelly
doughnut keeps the bird company.
The surf is pounding offshore like a sounding whale
ominous and white in the sharp afternoon sun shooting
over the stunted wind whipped spruce tops that line
the beach and the sea-grass bends with the tide brought
breeze and rustles almost as loudly as the waves
crashing out places for themselves in the rock.
The tide is out now and the ocean is allowing serenity
to creep in with the long advancing shadows
and the gently rippling tidal pools and the causeway
that joins the two islands is exposed and the gulls
are descending from the sunset in black relief like
rocks thrown at the sun and all Dwight said was
Jesus Christ, it's just the perfect place for clams.

Upon reading Therrien's two poems, Leo Connellan was moved to respond with the following:

Oh, Keith Therrien, what prevents Dwight from putting his metal traps down in th'water, computers erasing th'lobster so fast there isn't a claw mark? What has made our Dwight a sage who pronounces "it's just the perfect place for clams" what is he a tourist guide, not a Mainer!!? Why isn't Dwight clamming? What has happened to this native Mainer!, overwhelmed by invasion.... Keith, how's selling shoes goin' in the skinny economy of niggardly minds because I'll tell you the WASP's sting has long had its antidote and now Maine belongs to new people,, outsiders with money who come on about "th' rea-ul Maine.... where's that, Keith! Up near Houlton, maybe, Potato People driving Cadillacs good years and nothing lean, is it around Rockland out beyond th'Breakwater where the dead lie from violent ocean who made fish on industry, bone to bone, fish food, food human, the death equal and human toll as much as fish toll.... In your "red thin-napped carpet shoe store country" you after finding my "clear blue lobster-water country" for yourself, recognizing in yourself that there are those countries in what we are, where we come from in which what is right and wrong for us in the world and in ourselves could be universal. I thank you for your search, good poet Keith Therrien with soul and heart and real talent, thank you for a poem there are not many who come after me across Kittery Bridge, but, Keith Therrien when you lose your Blue Cross, Blue Shield and your girl friend will you write? Like the insurance companies ask their salesmen in the aptitude test "which is more important to you, selling insurance or your mother, do your children come before selling Insurance? That's the kind of game we're in, Keith, where of course you wouldn't really give up your family or your mother, but you just about would for poetry, wouldn't you Keith, wouldn't you!!? Keith remember what Oscar Wilde said "you better not want something, you just might get it,' Keith, and live like me nickel to nickel, penny pressed sweating Abe Lincoln, but every so often a poem no one can take away from you long after the sacrifice of your life for it, Keith Therrien, you are worth stars and shouts and joy and you are our hope. Now go find who you're writing for.... yes it is for yourself. Yes it is for me I write and then for you and Keith you and I write for people we will never meet.

The Dwight of both Keith's and Leo's poems is Dwight Rodgers of Corea, and what neither poet could have known was while Dwight does do some lobstering, he is fully employed at Young's Boat Yard and is the caretaker of summer places on Crowley's Island, including Easterly One, where another well-known poet, Amy Clampitt, has stayed for a number of years.

About that memorable evening in Hancock, just off Route One, Keith Therrien says, "I made a connection between creative impulse and the kinetic process of carrying out that impulse. Leo comes at you ragged and the sounds of his sentences are so long that you get the feeling that the words are nibbling at your ears. The sounds and rhythm nibble till your ears trickle blood and you know that you're getting something primal, raw, essential.

"That's what I saw the night he read underneath the rafters at the Pierre Monteux studio. A way of sounding which translated for me into a way of writing.

"Before I heard Leo, the first impulse of a poem so often got lost in my brain's unconscious intellectualizing and rationalizing and came out muddled and mediated like a strobe light through wax paper.

"The experience of that night changed my style and choice of diction and got me closer to poem as thing felt, seen and heard, not as poem considered and written.

"By leaving out conjunctions, articles, punctuation marks and even nouns and verbs, I was able to get the image in my mind's eye (which is where poetry starts) more accurately represented on paper. By slamming images and words, even sentences, closer together in a kenning sort of way, I was able to crosswire and go directly from impulse to product bridging the semantic no-man's-land between creative instinct and conventional orthography. This is basically a stream-of-consciousness approach, but if it works, don't label it. There is always time for consideration and editing afterward."

Thus, whether by simple accident or cosmic design, planned or unplanned, the bardic tradition continues here in Maine with the established poet handing on the tradition to the young poet. From the flickering fires of the mead hall in Old England to the barn-like web of rafters in Monteux Hall in Hancock, one generation speaks out dramatically to another, and is heard.

Editor's note:
When I finally located Keith Therrien and asked about his life "after Leo," I intended to summarize with a sentence or two, but his words are too memorable for summary:

Leo sent me a typed letter fairly quickly after he read my "Poet as

Shoesalesman" That poem grew out of conversation we had had one night as we rode with Sandy to a reading Leo did near Hancock Point.. I responded with a scorching poem, "Will I Still Write?" and we lost touch after that.

Up until that moment I had been a totally hopeless romantic about the value of art for arts sake and along comes this old cranky fart with a foul mouth and gravel in his throat who stood up under the rafters of this hall on the coast of Maine, my misunderstood home, and read his poetry of growing up in Maine (which I was trying to do) and blew everyone away with the honesty and earnestness of his words. It was a big moment for me and I never forgot it... He could do both: be commercial and transcendent at the same time and he had somehow reconciled all this. So I hope my poem communicates a little bit of that.

After UMaine, I fled the state in search of my father and bounced back and forth in that turmoil for several years holding several jobs such as janitor, and carpenter. I got married, had a daughter and started teaching high school English from which I've never graduated. Moved back to Maine with my daughter, taught English at Cony High School for five years, moved to NH with my second wife and her three children and now I teach in Massachusetts for the Department of Youth Services working with detained youth."

Keith has just submitted his latest poem to the *Puckerbruh Review.*

Leo Connellan: An Every-Man

Vivian Shipley

When he was seven years old, Leo Connellan's father called up from the bottom of the stairwell to him, "Your mother will not be here for Christmas." Later, aunts told Leo and his brother Jimmy that their mother had "to take care of someone else who needs her more than we do." To cope with the disappearance of his mother, Leo began writing poems and stories a year after Ida Elizabeth Carey Connellan died in 1935. Each year on her birthday, James Connellan, a devout Irish-Catholic, took his sons to visit their mother's grave. Leo's father, an attorney and a man who was known for over-explaining, did not explain his wife's death to his children, or allow them to grieve at the time of her death.

There was not much work for a lawyer during the Depression in Rockland, Maine, and James Connellan supported his two boys by serving as the first Irish Catholic postmaster in a Protestant state. His own father had come to Maine from Ireland to escape the famine. James Connellan was determined his family would not know hunger and he instilled in his young sons the fear of poverty created by the Depression. Because of his father's efforts, Leo never had to leave high school and go out on lobster fishing boats in order to eat. However, he learned about the hard lives of classmates who were not so fortunate when he spent summers pushing flakes of herring into the hot ovens of sardine factories. This identification with lobstermen, blueberry pickers and factory workers resulted in Leo's life long interest in the struggle for economic survival. In 1975, paying tribute to his father's work ethic, Leo dedicated *Another Poet in New York* to him: "This book is for my father, James Connellan, who backed me as long as he lived." However, Leo never recovered from his father's failure to explain the absence of his mother. In 1985, in the dedication to *The Clear Blue Lobster-Water Country*, Leo wrote: "This trilogy is for Ida Elizabeth Carey Connellan, who was my mother." The attempt to deal with her loss fueled his need to write poetry until the day he suffered a massive stroke at seventy-two.

In 1948, when Leo was nineteen and left the University of Maine to serve in the Army, he had already written two prize-winning poems. At Rockland High School, his teacher, Mrs. Ludwig, asked students to put a leaf on the poet Joyce Kilmer's tree. Leo wrote "The Leaf" and his teacher sent it to *Scholastic Scope* which was associated with The National High School Poetry Association. It won first prize and the certificate was put in the school library. Edna St. Vincent Millay was the other poet from Rockland, Maine to win this recognition.

The Leaf

I hang upon a tree in Spring
my beauty glowing bright.
Through Summer until early Fall
I never think of flight.
But as days wear on and on
I'm bored and yearn to fly.
So don't be scared if as you walk
you see a leaf go by

I spin, turn in splendor true
and somersaults I do.
As I go I wonder why
I cannot start anew, once more
to hang in beauty's eyes
a young, fragrant leaf.
To think that I've grown old and gray
is hardly my belief.

Some people think me burned in fire
or dust in slow decay.
When all the while I'm in the trees
from which I'll bud next May.

Written when Leo was sixteen, "The Leaf" was published in *Pleasure through Poetry* with another poem he wrote when he was seventeen,

"Someday I'll Be Dead." Leo placed them at the end of his *New and Collected Poems*.

Although Maine stayed at the heart of his poetry, Leo did not return to his native state. With a medical discharge from the Army after only six months of service, he went to Greenwich Village, where he associated with James Baldwin, Maxwell Bodenheim, Ruthven Todd and Henry Miller. Washing dishes, working as a soda jerk or pulling hand trucks in New York's garment district, Leo earned the thirty or forty dollars a week he needed to live and the manual work provided material for his poems. After two years, Leo became restless and to see the rest of the country first hand, he left New York City in 1952 to hitchhike through forty-one of the then forty-eight states. Often seeking help at the Salvation Army as he hoboed and panhandled, Leo met hardworking people who could not find jobs and learned that people were similar everywhere as they tried to maintain dignity while struggling with poverty. To record his life, Leo wrote stanzas of poems on paper napkins and the backs of envelopes during the eight years he spent traveling.

After leaving Maine in 1948, Leo had written only sporadically, but in 1961, he married Nancy Anderson. Now thirty-two, he wanted to write poetry as he had done as a teenager. In an interview done with William Packard for Issue 28 of *The New York Quarterly* which was included in Packard's *The Poet's Craft* (Paragon House, 1987), Leo said,

> I was dry probably from the time I was a young man, probably from 1947 through to about 1964. In other words, I had written some poems in high school, but no matter how many times I tried to get going I just couldn't do it. I couldn't do it in New York City, I couldn't seem to write when I was in various cities in the U.S. or Canada, and I sense that a lot of it, for me, had to do with the fact that I lived my adolescence probably between age twenty and thirty rather than between age twelve and twenty.

After their marriage, Leo and Nancy left for California (Nancy's home) where both worked briefly before returning east in 1964, where Leo tried to begin writing. Utilizing her education as a social worker,

Nancy supported him by becoming a caseworker in New York City. She left her position before Amy was born in 1967.

Leo started working for Old Town Corporation. Selling typewriter ribbons and carbon paper, he covered territory from Fort Kent, Maine to Baltimore, Maryland, and became Eastern Regional Sales Manager for Stationary Supplies. During those years, Leo established habits of writing that he would continue to follow, rising at 3:00 a.m. to do the wash and put on coffee in order to write from four to six. Carrying his manuscripts in his sales bag, when he had a break he would evaluate the morning's work. If his poem slapped him in the face, he would keep it. If it didn't, he crumpled it for the wastebasket. In the *NYQ* interview with Packard, Leo revealed, "I used to get anxiety attacks at the idea of having to go out and throw bull to sell something to feed my family—until the idea occurred to me in this getting up early that, really, quite honestly I was doing what I wanted to do *first* every day before I had to go and do what I must for The Man." In those early mornings, Leo created short poems like "Origins," "Tell Her That I fell," "Dark Horses Rushing," and "Watching Jim Shoulders."

In the interview with Packard, Leo provided insight into how a poem like "Watching Jim Shoulders" emerged: "I've had several periods in my life as a very heavy drinker. Once I was in Colorado Springs, Colorado as the guest of the Salvation Army and they got us indigents tickets to go see a rodeo. I went along to get along...Someone I had never heard of suddenly came lunging out of a corral on the back of a steer, and somebody said it was somebody called Jim Shoulders." Leo also told Packard, "My book *Massachusetts Poems: Coming to Cummington to Take Kelly* was written during the two months that I lived in a motel room while at the company headquarters where I worked in Pinebrook, New Jersey."

In 1970, Leo was awarded a grant from the National Endowment for the Arts and another in October, 1972 from Connecticut Commission on the Arts. Drawing on his years in Maine, his two years in Greenwich Village and the eight years he spent hitchhiking America, Leo wrote unburdened by politics or ideology. Writing for common men about the never-ending fight to eat and keep a roof over a family's head, he infused vigor into his poetry with the reality of detail. Leo trusted others to discover his poem because the work was based on actual situations and people, entwined with imaginative forays that used reality as a stepping-off point. Leo always acknowledged the imaginative aspect in his work; he and Nancy often wondered why some readers assumed, incorrectly, that all the details in his poems were factual.

Poems he wrote as a result of the NEA and CCA awards formed Leo's first two books. Located in New Haven, John Baringer published Leo's first book in 1974, *Penobscot Poems* (New Quarto Editions). In it Leo expressed his gratitude to William Wallace Davidson for publishing "Dark Horses Rushing" in *The Georgia Review*. Another poem in the collection, "Watching Jim Shoulders," had been published in *The Nation*.

The following year, Leo's second book, *Another Poet in New York* (Living Poets Press, 1975), was published. A letter in front of the collection from Karl Shapiro to Leo dated July 16, 1951, shows how long Leo had been exchanging ideas about the poems with Shapiro who wrote:

> A poem is all by itself and when you're writing it, it has nothing to do with you. It's your solution of it that counts. You fight for it, you lay traps. You cheat, lie, starve, fast, go off the deep end, come back, but in the long run, if you're lucky, you have it where you wanted it—on paper. But there's no satisfaction to it at all except one... that you did something that was a purely dispassionate act. You made an anonymous gift to an anonymous recipient. When it's all over, the poem will be as foreign to you as to anyone else. It will never be something you said or thought or felt, only something made out of your natural yearning for form.

The title of this second book and a poem, "Lament for Federico Garcia Lorca," acknowledge the influence of *Poeta En Nueva York*. Celebrating old relationships and lost loves, Leo's poems depict the struggle of displaced American veterans, the ones who came home from World War II totally confused by the revolution in sexual roles created by women who were sitting on the front porch when their men left and working in factories when they returned. Settings for poems are drawn from Manhattan with its subways, the Staten Island Ferry and violent streets. From this volume, William Packard published "The Moon Now Flushed" in *The New York Quarterly*. Stanley Kunitz awarded the poem the first Lucille Medwick Poetry Prize. Richard Eberhart summed up the strength of *Another Poet in New York* in the cover quote: "Everybody interested in modern poetry should read the passionate work of Leo Connellan. He speaks with the authority of experience, profound knowledge for the heart, and a deep realization of man's predicament. His poetry is vital and strong."

Years after his eight year journey through forty-one states, Leo was able to assemble a third book, *Crossing America* (Penman Press, 1976), in less than three weeks from the stanzas, lines and notes he had written while he traveled America in the 1950's. Again, Richard Eberhart commented on the strength of this volume in the Preface: "Leo Connellan does not belong to the main stream of university poetry for university educated readers, but to another mainstream of American consciousness whose textbook is raw life. The merit of his poems is in their commonness. He does not philosophize on why things are as they are, are thus and so. He writes poetry of direct power without linguistic embellishments."

In addition to William Packard, another editor who figured significantly in Leo's career was Paul Zimmer at the University of Pittsburgh Press. Zimmer pulled together poetry from Leo's first two books to form *First Selected Poems*. Published in 1976, the book represented the work, except for *Crossing America*, that Leo valued from his early years of writing. Praise was abundant for Zimmer's collection of Leo's work. Robert Penn Warren wrote, "How much more poetry there is here than in most of the books I have read for a year." Richard Wilbur added, "There is wiriness in the movement of these poems that I like."

Buoyed by the favorable critical reception of *First Selected Poems,* Leo returned to writing about Maine people of his youth. The hopes, dashed dreams of blueberry pickers, the longing for love among fishing girls abused by lobster men who had turned to alcohol for consolation were the topics of poems that formed *Death in Lobster Land* (Great Raven Press, 1978). In the Foreword, Hubert Selby Jr. observed, "These poems are a celebration of survival by a heart that prevailed."

A year after publishing *Death in Lobster Land,* Leo lost his job selling stationary supplies because nineteen manufacturers went out of business, and he was unable to make mortgage payments on the family home in Clinton, Connecticut. Because of the equity Leo and Nancy had in their home, they were able to sell it, pay off debts, and have money to live on for a time. They took a trip to England and France to visit friends, and returned to Connecticut and where they moved to a small Norwich apartment. When Leo began drinking again, Nancy found full-time employment as a caseworker. During that time Leo swept floors and did substitute teaching. After four years, Leo stopped drinking and stayed sober until his death in 2001. His life changed in 1982, when at fifty-four, Leo won the Poetry Society of America's Shelley Memorial Award.

During these difficult years of 1979-82, Leo wrote the first two books of the trilogy he considered to be his major life-work: *The Clear Blue Lobster-Water Country* (Harcourt Brace Jovanovich, 1985). The first part, *Massachusetts Poems: Coming to Cummington to Take Kelly*, was published in 1981 by Alexander Harvey, Editor of Hollow Spring Press. The second part, *Shatterhouse*, was published by Hollow Spring Press in 1983. Leo added the title poem to these two books to complete his trilogy. In the Foreword of *The Clear Blue Lobster-Water Country*, Sydney Lea commented on Leo's continued role as an outsider:

> We are late into the American Century, and by now most of our poets have associated themselves with colleges and universities...The author of this trilogy is in this matter, as in many, exceptional. He has for years operated not only without academic tenure but also without any institutional ratification of his right to be a writer. Leo Connellan's only *tenure,* in fact has been his fierce inner conviction that patience, courage, and honesty must result in the only poetry worth its name, and by corollary that language manipulated to please one's *superiors* is necessarily twisted into something worse than failure....How tempting it must have been for Connellan—in a life so harrowingly difficult that it would be pretentious for a middle-class poet like me to anatomize it—to sink precisely into such self-serving cynicism.

In the trilogy, American social values are collapsing, and contemporary society has drifted widely from its origins. The central character,

Boppledock, learns that it is up to individuals to affirm their own humanity. In Book I, Boppledock begins to question democratic values because he fantasizes that he watched a fixed race on Patriot's Day. Concurrent with this struggle is Bop's attempt to make things right with his real father. Ultimately, he recognizes that the past cannot be redeemed. By Book II, Bop has broken down and is in the kind of treatment available to people who do not have Blue Cross/Blue Shield. Bop comes to realize that he, like all people, has the ability to cure himself. In Book III, Boppledock concludes that if he could achieve selflessness combined with usefulness to others, he would be willing to leave this life. The trilogy succeeds in conveying how common man can keep integrity and value in the face of overwhelming loss by retaining the capacity for love.

Again, critics responded warmly to Leo's poetry. On March 1, 1985, Christina Robb in the *Boston Globe* said: "He writes with candor so naked and new born it makes you love the fighters and lovers, almost because of their helpless ignorance and lust. He invests these people, his own people, with all his attention and entitlement, as if they were the only people in the world, in his eyes and so in ours. They become clues to the mysteries that lead us on in life." In *The New York Times Book Review* on July 14, 1985, R.W. Flint summed up the collection's achievement: "Mr. Connellan makes strong unspoken appeals for the reader's imaginative assistance. Some poets do all our work for us, and more. But this one's writing comes all sad and shaggy, rowdy, rough and ready, from deep regions of the now declassified creative unconscious."

Connellan's next book, *New and Collected Poems* (Paragon House, 1989), contains poems written between 1944 and 1988 which reveal how his work evolved after he, like Boppledock, realized that inner revelations about self, some achieved in highly imaginative meanderings, can allow others to discover truths about themselves. An example of a poem in the collection is "Dark Horses Rushing." Published by William Davidson in *The Georgia Review* (XXII, No. 1, Spring, 1968), this poem, written the night Leo's only child, Amy Charlotte, was born, explores the miracle of creation and life that the work probes and ultimately celebrates. Hayden Carruth in his essay, "Narrative Anyone?" (*Parnassus Poetry in Review*, Volumes 17, No. 2 & 18, No.1, 1990), echoed Sydney Lea's comments about Leo as an outsider:

> Internationalism and elitism have always gone hand in hand in the American arts. Connellan has resolutely distanced himself from this, while at the same time and just as resolutely he has denied any affiliation with prairie sentimentalism or proletarian utilitarianism. He is a poet of the American working class who is as sophisticated as any of the elite but who has retained working-class values as the nucleus of his program....Like McGrath's work, however, Connellan's has not been much acknowledged by the Modernist critical establishment—elitist, internationalist, Vendlerist—until now. I hope this will change.

The biography on *New and Collected Poems* notes that by 1989, Leo had become the Poet-In Residence at Eastern Connecticut State University. He was then named Poet-in Residence for the entire Connecticut State University System, a position he held until his death. Because of the financial stability the job with the CSU System gave him, Leo, Nancy, and Amy were able to move to a townhouse in Sprague, Connecticut.

In the second book Leo dedicated to his father, *Provincetown and Other Poems* (Willimantic, Connecticut: Curbstone Press, 1995), cover quotes indicate the work continued to garner words of high praise from American's major poets. Karl Shapiro noted, "Leo Connellan has retained his soul and voice." Richard Wilbur calls him "one of our most distinctive poets." In Rebecca Bearardy's interview for Curbstone Press about *Provincetown* (http://www.curbstone.org/ainterview.cfm?AuthID=73) Leo continued to emphasize his status as an outsider:

> On my tombstone, if anybody ever bothers to write such a thing, I'd like to be called an every-man...We have a history in America of having clubs. Robert Penn Warren created something called the Fugitive Group at Vanderbilt University. I don't know what they were fugitives from. They were all wealthy and academic scholars and some of them like Randall Jarrell, Robert Penn Warren and Allen Tate could write great poetry, but in order to get it noticed they felt they had to call themselves something so everyone would notice them. There are poets like Jack Hirschman, Tom McGrath, Muriel Rukeyser, Gwendolyn Brooks, and Leo Connellan who just wrote their work. They tried to write the best poetry of which they were capable without being identified with some group.

In addition to the financial security provided by the CSU System, public recognition did come to Leo. After James Merrill's death, he was appointed the second Poet Laureate of Connecticut in 1996. Leo also made a film for Maine Public Television, and was awarded a doctorate of humane letters from University of Maine in May, 1998. Even with this recognition, Leo continued to identify himself with the blue-collar world that had provided constant subject matter and inspiration for his poems. In July, 1998, he told *The Hartford Courant*'s interviewer for *Northeast*, "I'm not an academic. I'm not in the club. I'm a working man who writes poems."

Leo collected his early work about Maine and the time he spent crossing America into his final two books: *Short Poems/City Poems* 1944-1998 (Hanover Press, 1999) and *Maine Poems* (Blackberry Press, 1999). Poems in his two final collections were crafted in years Leo had so much difficulty in overcoming childhood loss of his mother, alcoholism and continuing economic adversity.

In 2000, a year before his death, Leo was named as one of the hundred most important writers in Maine's history. As Connecticut's Poet Laureate and Poet-in-Residence for the Connecticut State University System, Leo maintained his life-long writing schedule while he drove around Connecticut sharing his love of poetry with young writers. Two or three times a week, Leo traveled to high schools, middle schools and universities to lead workshops. Dr. William Cibes, Chancellor of the CSU System, commented, "We have files and files of thank-you letters from students and parents who had worked with Leo. If there was one theme to those letters, it was that suddenly the students were able to understand poetry and use it to express their feelings." On February 24, 2001, after Leo's death, his daughter, Amy, commented in The *Hartford Courant*:

> He was going to help children understand and create and use words as their way of creating, and he wanted to teach them self-esteem. He was determined that he was going to do what he could to have children have confidence and believe in themselves. He believed that poetry and art are for everyone, not just for the elite and privileged, but for the kid in the barrio as much as the kid raised in a comfortable suburban home.

When a stroke felled him on February 15, 2001, in death as in life, Leo's mind, his spirit went ahead, and the body followed as it must on February 22, 2001, when he died at William W. Backus Hospital in Norwich. As they had been each day of the life the three of them shared, Nancy and Amy were there to ease his passage with their love, with the touch of their hands. Funeral services were held for Leo in Norwich's St. Patrick's Cathedral at Nancy's request because she felt a Mass of Christian Burial was the only fitting farewell for Leo who was Catholic in his heart. After reading his poems, Monsignor Anthony Rosaforte came to agree that throughout his life, Leo loved the church his body was returned to at the last. During the service, placing Leo's *New and Collected Poems* on the altar, Monsignor Rosaforte emphasized the impact of his mother's death on the young boy of seven. Noting that Leo never got any satisfactory understanding about death from his strict Irish-Catholic father or the culture surrounding his family, Rosaforte helped mourners understand how hard that must have been on a mind that was always questioning. Monsignor Rosaforte concluded, "No one could be that angry at the church, unless he loved it." Resting on the altar as the last work in *New and Collected Poems*, the poem Leo wrote in 1946 when he was seventeen reflected the lifelong tension that Monsignor Rosaforte memorialized:

Someday I'll Be Dead

Someday I'll be dead
and all of you will mourn,
not because I'm dead
because another one of you is gone.

You'll be thinking of your turn
just around the bend
where bowed beneath your Maker's feet
you will meet your end.

Someday I'll be gone
and you will have my cares
like puppets on a string dancing
up on makeshift airs
you'll wonder when your turn will come.

We're quite a marionette
a show for all to see
and when I'm dead and gone
you'll remember me.

Not as one you loved or knew,
as one you needed to get
your performance through.

Born in Portland, Maine on November 30, 1928, when he died on February 22, 2001, Leo Connellan made Connecticut his final home. On Monday, February 26, 2001, in the quiet country setting of Plains Cemetery in Franklin, Connecticut, Leo's body found the peace he had sought for much of his life. Like a leaf he wrote about at sixteen that stays in the tree until it buds in May, his spirit remains in words he left about the loss of another:

Scott Huff

Think tonight of sixteen
year old Scott Huff of
Maine driving home fell asleep at
the wheel, his car sprang awake
from the weight of his foot head on
into a tree. God, if you need him
take him asking me to believe in
you because there are yellow buttercups,
salmon for my heart in the rivers,
fresh springs of ice cold water running away.
You can have all these back for Scott Huff.

from *Negative Capability*, 1994

Connellan in Performance

David Shippee

Leo Connellan came into my life not as a poet. Our introduction came one day over the telephone in his role as breadwinner-insurance telemarketer, rather than bard. This was at a time when his appointment as poet-in-residence for the Connecticut State University system had been stashed in a bureaucratic limbo.

State governments, in their budgeting process, have a way of letting the arts slip into dark places. When dollars get tight artists lose their place in the sun to more politically correct flowers. Deputy sheriffs and lotto machine repairmen become better uses of the taxpayer's grudging dollars than finger paints, or a well-turned phrase.

It was in this context that Leo had been forced to take a job hustling point of sale appointments at local kitchen tables for an insurance agent and what caused him to ring my phone in particular. A mutual friend, named Andy Thibault, who is an assistant bureau chief for the *Hartford Courant*, had suggested to Leo I might be of help to him in his insurance mode, since my 30 years in that business qualified me as a "survivor."

I filled Connellan in on the family insurance scene as best I could, and then our conversation turned to writing. Leo sketched in the broad facts of his life to that point, and in the talk that followed we realized we had more friends in common than just Andy, and better yet, we shared a lot of what modern day educators lump into something called "cultural literacy." We hit it off.

This initial conversation blossomed into daily phone calls, shared Chinese vegetables, swapping of obscure books, and a pretty comfortable friendship between two aging salesmen who regularly kid each

other that "we've seen it all."
To have the man tell me that he is a poet was one thing. To read his words in print was another. Neither the simple statement of what he is, nor the reading of the published evidence prepared me for the ultimate showcase of Connellan's poetry—a Connellan poetry reading. Leo has read his poetry at Dartmouth. He has read at Yale. He has been the honored guest of the New England Poetry Society, and upon winning the Shelley Memorial Poetry Prize, Leo's phone rang with invitations to read from all corners of the map.

My first glimpse of the poet, as performer, came in front of a group of high school students in Waterford, Connecticut. It was magic, and it always is. It doesn't matter if his reading is in front of tenured professors of the Ivy League, or with a group of former high school dropouts in Carol McGarry's adult-ed night school class. The result is consistently rewarding and eagerly applauded. The man is a rare mix of reclusive writer and public performer of his own play.

So many practitioners of the studio arts languish in their obscurity because they are unable, or unwilling, to peddle their wares in the marketplace. Not so Connellan. A typical Connellan reading starts out with the uninitiated seated in the folding chairs, trying to figure out what the white-haired, rumpled looking poet in front of them can possibly add to their day. Veterans of such readings need never wonder, or ask those questions.

Leo touches his industrial strength plastic eyeglasses to the bridge of his nose, looks the room over, and starts to speak. He addresses everyone in very polite terms, and you are either "ladies and gentlemen" or you are "young women and young men." He seems tentative, and overly concerned that he may be disinvited if he steps on any toes. It is an opening act not unlike the beggar at the feast, or maybe akin to the late Professor Irwin Corey, who bumbled his way onto the Ed Sullivan television show on Sunday nights long ago.

What's really happening in these first, seemingly hesitant, moments is that Leo is sizing up his room. The salesman is measuring the prospects in front of him and probing their defenses. Then he makes his move. His voice takes on a timber that is anything but reticent. The images tumble out frequently dark and troubled. The narrative takes wing, and the listeners are suddenly being played like the flutes and oboes they are Connellan's orchestra. Force and conviction, craft and skill, all converge in his carefully sculpted words. Every eye follows the poet as he strides back and forth, book in hand and held out at arm's length, or maybe he's just sitting.

New York in the 60's. The cutting bite of a bitter mid-west coldsnap. Drugs and booze. The unqualified love of a man for a woman, and hers for him. All these snippets of memory and emotion lie in a growing heap at the reader's feet as the words literally spew from the page he is speaking, and they are his, those listening people that were perplexed by his earlier, meeker, self. Connellan has made another score!

To say that Leo Connellan is a writer is to understate the case. To say that he was once a salesman is to deny a part of the man that still lives, instinctively. When these two aspects of Connellan fuse at a public reading of his poetry, work that you originally recognized as exceptional becomes irresistible. It never fails to happen.

from *The New Haven Advocate*, October, 1978

Review of *Death in Lobster Land*: Poet Portrays 'Injustices of the Human Heart'

Wally Swist

> *A poem is an anonymous gift to an anonymous recipient;*
> *and you're finished with it, it doesn't belong to you anymore,*
> *it belongs to someone else.*
> —Karl Shapiro, in a letter to Leo Connellan

Leo Connellan is a poet who has weathered a 14-year silence from writing, a bout with alcoholism, and a number of nine-to-five jobs as a traveling salesman. He portrays his home state of Maine, where the winters can be as harsh as the economy, with a verbal crispness, a compassion. His poems are funereal, tragic and resonant.

"So many of my poems are about Maine because that's where I come from. They're working men, about the injustices of the human heart," says Connellan, who at 50 has just published his eighth collection of poems, *Death In Lobster Land*.

You don't have to come from Maine to appreciate his work. Nor do you have to be an academic, although Connellan is an exceptional craftsman. His poems. lure you with their lyricism, then snap shut like a lobster trap. Take "Scott Huff" for example:

> Think tonight of sixteen
> year old Scott Huff of
> Maine driving home fell asleep at
> the wheel, his car sprang awake
> from the weight of his foot head on
> into a tree; God, if you need him
> take him asking me to believe in
> you because there are yellow buttercups,
> salmon for my heart in the rivers,

fresh springs of ice cold water running away.
You can have all these back for Scott Huff.

After attending the University Of Maine, Connellan took his chances spinning around the country like a chip played on a roulette wheel. For Connellan, Maine would be a place he'd always come back to, that would draw him back again and again, but New York City proved to be his primary stomping grounds from the mid '50s through the early '60s.

When he lived in New York, he'd sell carbon paper and typewriter ribbons between 8 a.m. and 2 p.m., then go to the Limelight Cafe on Sheridan Square to write.

"I made it an atmosphere where I could write," he says. "In that din and over cups of coffee I realized time was passing me by, and that I didn't have any excuses left for not writing. I embraced it."

"My career as writer began by what I thought writing might be," Connellan continues. "The trick of writing is simplicity. The thing to do is edit. Once the idea is clear, get rid of excess words. Excess words reveal the writer is bluffing behind nothing to say. I don't rush. The poem will be done when it is. But the minute you have to explain it you're writing prose."

Finally *Penobscot Poems* was published by New Quarto Editions in 1974. Then a quick succession of books followed—*Another Poet In New York* (Living Poets Press), *First Selected Poems* (University of Pittsburgh Press), *Crossing America* (Penmaen Press), *Seven Short Poems* (Western Maryland College Writers Union), and this year, from Great Raven Press of Fort Kent, Maine, *Death In Lobster Land*.

"Writing is something you can't help yourself from doing," he says now after his years of struggle. "It is everything to me, and I knew I *could* write if I didn't die from bad luck or from drinking."

Connellan is an elegist, and *Death In Lobster Land* is his best work to date. "It is the book I always wanted to write," he says. The book contains many long poems such as "By The Blue Sea," "Edwin Coombs" and " Amelia, Mrs. Brooks Of My Old Childhood"—painful reminiscences knotted like the callused hands of the fishermen and factory workers that they both criticize and eulogize. They are raw and overpowering, compelling rereading after rereading. They have so much life compressed in them that they throb.

Simultaneous with the publication of *Death In Lobster Land,* a movie has just been released, *Leo Connellan At 50,* and will shortly be aired on public and cable television. Created by Eikon Associates, Inc., the film runs 32 minutes, and is complemented by the still photos of photographer Herschel E. Grubb, interfacing Connellan reading six of his poems.

"There are two ways that we write," says Connellan. "Either we are born brilliant or something disturbs us." He claims that "all good writing is realized by us because of what the writer has written for the reader to fill in. This gives us the feeling that we've had something to do with its accomplishment. I think this is the secret of art."

Leo Connellan has succeeded in what he set off to do so many years ago in Rockland, Maine, his hometown, where he feels "it was an accomplishment to be born there, grow up, and leave."

In his work he fulfills his own credo—including and disturbing the reader.

from *Connecticut Magazine*, 1995

THE LIFE OF THE POET

Andy Thibault

During 50 years of writing poetry, Leo Connellan has kept the faith and kept working hard. Now he's reaping some rewards.

Hear the poet who talks over the backyard fence, to the next guy on the assembly line, to the clerk, to the chambermaid:

Father, we'll meet again.
You can tell me you love me then.

Father is dead. Planted. Gone forever. But the poet, Leo Connellan, is not giving up. Not just yet. He constructs a foot race in which he defeats the bully who terrorized him as a child.

For you. Father, I imagined up a contest.
Sought out an adversary where none exists,
To win your heart beyond the grave where I
Never had it here.
Will my only child, daughter,
seek me out as I see you out!?

Now the academics and poetry elite are listening to Connellan as well. El Bardo The Legend, as his admirers like to call him, has developed a following as New England's working-class poet, and at age 67 is producing some of his best work. His 12th book, *Provincetown & Other Poems*, was scheduled for a second printing after only eight months on the bookstore shelves. His 50 years of work represent a triumph of his will to be a responsible, providing father, a husband and a poet. The poems themselves are a celebration of perseverance, day-to-day survival, and a heart that refuses to quit.

Connellan, who lives with his wife and daughter in a modest apartment in the old mill town of Sprague in eastern Connecticut near

Norwich, is also a top contender to succeed the late James Merrill as Connecticut's poet laureate. More than a few players in the poetry power structure see an intriguing evolution as a so-called proletariat writer is considered to replace Merrill, an erudite heir to a Wall Street fortune. Among those who have put Connellan's name before the Connecticut commission of the Arts is poet James Laughlin of Norfolk, the editor and publisher for Ezra Pound. Laughlin says he was moved by Connellan's "ability to establish a meaningful, even a colloquial relationship with his readers. As a poet myself," he added, "I envy him his directness."

Also in Connellan's corner is Sydney Lea, editor of the *New England Review*. Lea suggested to the arts commission that is now time for Connellan, a "more vernacular, populist, even Whitmanian" writer, to be Connecticut's poet laureate.

In person, Connellan cuts a large and complex figure. When he gives a reading, he enters a room tentatively. He is certain of his work, but not his audience. He usually begins by making small talk, feeling out the crowd.

"I was very skeptical when I first met the guy," says David Wilson of Bantam, an investment and insurance adviser. "I'm not one who reads books or takes time to smell the roses. But he basically drew me in."

They met at a recent business luncheon in Litchfield, where Connellan was the guest speaker. As he often does, the poet began the session by making fun of his own prodigious girth, comparing himself at one point to a "pregnant water buffalo." He also wondered aloud if he truly did have anything to offer, then spoke of his military service and his abiding belief in the United States as the land of opportunity for a hustler.

"What sustained some of us during the Depression," Connellan said, "was the belief that the common man could pursue happiness. Those of us who believed this actually believed you could go out and do whatever you wanted. I chose to be a poet. I took my chances."

You could see him sizing up the room, like a salesman measuring the prospects before him. His close friend David Shippee, a New London insurance salesman, says Connellan does this at every reading, whether it's at Harvard, Brooklyn Polytech or an adult education class in Groton.

"He's got that salesman's knack for reaching the audience," Shippee says. "It's called street smarts. Wherever he goes, he ends up enthralling people."

Connellan told the group of Litchfield Rotarians that his mother died when he was 7, and that he has spent his entire life wondering what she would think of him. While on the subject of motherhood, he read from a news story about an aborted fetus that had been placed in another woman's womb. It was a story that had led him to write a poem, which he called "Let's Fall in Love."

My mother was an abortion.
No, I mean it, an unborn fetus
eggs planted in a hippopotamus
so if I seem an animal
There's this good reason
but I'm empty from not knowing
my real mom who was never here
so I could be antisocial or distant
or in so much need I'm overwhelming.
Should I love my birth mom
or my mom mom?

"Much of my work is written out of what disturbed me," Connellan says later, over coffee at a Torrington coffeehouse. He wrote his first poems at age 17, as a high school student in Rockland, Maine. Two poems won national prizes and were published in *Scholastic Scope*. When he saw his plaque placed in the trophy case next to one for the football team, he decided poetry was for him.

Many of his classmates would become farmers, factory workers or lobstermen. He spent summers working in a sardine factory. From Maine he went to Greenwich Village, where his circle of associates at places like the White Horse Tavern included Allen Ginsberg, Henry Miller, James Baldwin and Maxwell Bodenheim.

"I was trying to get away from a small town," he recalls. "I went to

New York in 1949 and I happened to meet a lot of well-known people. I sat with Dylan Thomas in the White Horse Tavern when I couldn't write. I think he was almost revolted by what I showed him as a poem."

But he was a decent guy. I didn't know Dylan personally as a friend, but we knew each other the way you know people who you sit and drink with and see all the time. He was working man's human being. He never went in the place and bragged about who he was. He never postured. He was a great artist, but he had a sense of the world. He didn't flout it. The guys who push you around are third-raters."

Connellan liked much of what he found in New York. "Greenwich Village was a place to hide," he says, "and it was wonderful not to have your father looking over your shoulder. You could do anything you felt like—you could drink too much, you could make love too much, you could vanish, you could work when you wanted to work. Greenwich Village was the place where I sort of grew up."

At length, though, he grew restless. In 1953, like others of his age and inclinations, he set out to see America. Working menial jobs and writing notes and poems on paper napkins and the backs of envelopes, he hitchhiked through all 48 states.

"I had no money and I wanted to see my country," he recalls. "I wanted to convince myself that people sneeze in Alabama the way they sneeze in Torrington. I knew eventually I was going to stop somewhere, probably New York or Connecticut or Maine. I knew that I was going to stop and try to write."

But even after he came back east, he couldn't seem to get off the road. In 1961, after marrying Nancy Anderson, a social worker, Connellan began a career as a traveling salesman. For 17 years he sold stationery supplies from Maine to Maryland—"a lot of selling and motels and restaurants," as he puts it now. He wrote his poems on the road, rising at 3 a.m.

"I went to work but I wrote every day," he says. "Sometimes I didn't know what I was doing, but I just did it. I was like a ballplayer who bats a ball in a vacant lot and everybody wonders what he's doing.

They wonder. They wonder if he's crazy. One day they let him play in the game. He's been hitting that ball so long that when the guy throws it, he knocks it over the fence and everybody says, 'How did you do that?' Because he got his swing, he got his motion, he knew what he was doing. And he practiced. That's the kind of life I've lived. I wrote poems from 1947 to 1974 before I got my first book."

Encouraged by William Packard of *The New York Quarterly*, Connellan published *Another Poet* in New York in 1975. That volume focuses on the struggles of veterans after World War II. A second book, *Crossing America*, followed a year later. Earlier, Packard had published Connellan's poem, "The Moon Now Flushed," in the *Quarterly*. The poem recounted part of what he had seen and felt on the road 20 years earlier. It begins:

Across American the
young men were
throwing their
serial numbers away,
and some were sticking
their thumbs out along
the highways hitting
the cities broke.
And always Fry Cook
and Counterman jobs in
the cafeteria chains or
loading freight cars
with empty beer cans at
the American Can Company.
You learned to buy and
carry with you your own
skillet that scrambled eggs
would never stick in, which
could put you out of work,
and a small pot for poached
eggs, your own equipment,
black tie and cummerbund
Meant an
immediate meal for you,
meant money now.

Like Steinbeck, Connellan confers dignity, honor and meaning on the dispossessed. The denizens of Cannery Row are first cousins to Connellan's Knights of the Round Table—the lobsterman, the grunt soldier, the waitress at the diner.

Emily Grosholz, one of America's highly regarded poets and a professor of philosophy at the University of Pennsylvania, is a fan of Connellan's. "Connellan writes much better than Charles Bukowski," Grosholz says, "but with unrelenting fierceness fueled by what he has seen of the country's underside."

"Motel," a selection from *Provincetown & Other Poems*, shows the poet staying in a luxury motel during a book tour, spending a good deal of his time with the staff.

> This is a new one from the most famous luxury chain,
> just opened, with a cheap rate to fill
> rooms and give staff practice... that
>
> succeeds because the help's picked from immigrants.
> Cocktail waitress forced to wear outfit that
> makes her look stripped, fired if they catch
>
> her chewing or her mouth looking like it's got
> anything in it but her tongue.

Connellan continued to publish and find new admirers—and deal with persistent demons. In his major work, a trilogy called *The Clear Blue Lobster-Water Country*, the main character tries to reconcile with his dead father. The character, Boppledock, is looking for happiness, "to become whole again." Boppledock is also tormented by the prospect of repeating his father's mistakes with his own child.

Connellan admits to an obsession with the absent father, not an uncommon theme in American literature. "I loved my father very much," he says. "He was a very hard man to get along with. He lived in the American Depression. He was a lawyer, and all of a sudden the market crashed and he really couldn't practice law. All of a sudden his dreams were gone."

"I had a very hard time dealing with him. He did his best, functionally. I think he gave up on me a long time before I reached manhood. When I told him I wanted to go to New York, he was relieved. He didn't know how to deal with me because I wanted to be a poet. I don't even know how much my father wanted me when I was born. How do you ever know that?" "My brother told me the other day that Dad would be proud of me, and I find that hard to accept."

Perhaps Connellan's own experience helped him resolve to head off that dilemma with his own child. "There has never been a time," Connellan's daughter Amy says, "When I didn't know that nothing I could ever do or say would ever make him stop loving me."

The Clear Blue Lobster-Water Country earned Connellan the Shelley Memorial Award in 1982, placing him among the ranks of fellow Shelley winners Anne Sexton, Robert Penn Warren and e.e. cummings. Ironically, the publication of his work and his growing fame as a poet came at a difficult time for Connellan; the stationery-supply company he'd represented had gone out of business, and he was left without a regular source of income. He had to scramble for a job.

"I was out of work at 48 years of age," he recalls, "and I was reduced to sweeping stairs, climbing three flights of stairs on two sides of 21 buildings for $35 a week. I was reduced to substitute teaching for $25 a day."

It wasn't until one day in 1985, at a graduation exercise in Norwich, that the superintendent of schools noticed a highly regarded poet among the ranks of his substitute teachers. A few well-placed words soon landed him a job as poet-in-residence for the Connecticut state university system. In that post, Connellan works out of an office at Eastern Connecticut State University, lecturing there and at Central in new Britain, Southern in New Haven and Western in Danbury. He has also devised an outreach program for middle schools and high schools, often working one-on-one with difficult students.

At Torrington Middle School, where students read Connellan's poems about subjects such as garbage trucks with fondness and robust laughter, teacher Rosemary Reynolds credits the poet with introducing the students to creative expression. "It stayed with them all year," Reynolds says of a weeklong visit by Connellan in 1994. "Their writing became much more image filled."

"Every time I write a poem now," says 13-year-old Torrington Middle School student Elena Forzani, "I look for an image that is different than anyone else's. I feel freer. I feel I don't have to please anyone else."

Some critics now mention Connellan in the same breath as Henry Wadsworth Longfellow, Edna St. Vincent Millay and Edwin Arlington Robinson, and he has been nominated three times for the Pulitzer Prize.

"Leo's writing his best work now in his 60's, just like Yeats did," says Sandy Taylor of Willimantic, whose Curbstone Press published *Provincetown & Other Poems*. "You get those Rambo types who have a big flash and disappear, but Leo's been steady and consistent. The thing that impresses us is that his work remains rooted in the earth and daily life; he reaches out into the community, rather than orbiting in his own ego or writing to other poets."

Connellan finds satisfaction in his work, and in the recognition, too. "It's an American fantasy to be a movie star or to be Michael Jordan or to be something like that. But by the time the prizes come, what they mean to you is that maybe someone will hire you because they're reassured."

"I'm glad I have the Shelley Memorial Award, but it was never the reason that I wrote. If I never get the Pulitzer Prize, I won't stop writing. It would be nice to be honored, and to be acknowledged but what's more important to me at 67 years of age is that I don't have Alzheimer's—God willing, I won't get that. And I still have a wish to write. That's what's really important."

That, and to know he has finally found acceptance back in Maine, where he started out, where his doubts and his father's doubts disturbed him so deeply all those years ago. In Orono, where he worked on poems with a group of high school football players, they started a Leo Club, complete with T-shirts. This fall, he read at Bowdoin College and College of the Atlantic, in Bar Harbor.

"The big thing for me about being invited to read in Maine," Connellan says, "is a boy named maybe Young Leo left Maine at 19 to try to become some kind of writer. We have to make a dream to keep ourselves going but you write anyway—not for wealth, not for security, but because you cannot help it. You're a writer, whether anyone else thinks you are. Nobody asked you to be, nobody sent for you, perhaps few care what you do. Only you care, only you. And that's enough.

"Perhaps if you do it, you do get a job, some notice. I've been lucky enough to have a wonderful wife and daughter and cats, and get invitations to come home and read my work—and that's a lot."

On the Phone with Leo

Daniel Tobin

I never met Leo Connellan, not in person, though the first time I spoke with him long distance on the phone he sounded in manner if not in accent like one of my father's cronies at Muse's Bar in Brooklyn—all bluntness and bluster, and the kind of indefatigable demeanor that would have led my father to observe "He's a real character." My father would have recognized the utterly unique configuration of attributes and idiosyncrasies, being himself a real character, blue-collar to the bone, and therefore a man incapable of posing which means, of course, his own originality was completely invisible to him. I suspect this was true of Leo as well, since in those few conversations I had with him we spoke with an unguarded immediacy about poets and poetry that is hard to encounter either in the rarified air of the academy or in the ego-driven milieu of Poetry Biz. I heard the Maine coast wind inside his vowels, despite his having lived in New York, in my own Brooklyn and now in Connecticut, different from my father's raw Brooklynese that could rhyme "oil" with "pearl," but the same no nonsense working-class view of things, the same sense of having been tutored in what my father called The School of Hard Knocks.

Leo Connellan of course understood both the world of business and hard knocks and the world of reading and intellect, and would have recognized the muse among the denizens of Muse's Bar. I had come to know his poems over the years, despite their largely small press productions, and had come to admire both their stark, unsentimental vision and their blunt but sophisticated music. I wanted to include a necessary few of them in the project I had decided to undertake, an anthology of Irish American poetry from the 18th Century to the present—the largest anthology of its kind compiled in over a hundred years—and had written him, along with other contemporaries, asking that he contribute several poems from which I would choose. I asked each living poet for eight to ten poems, as well as suggestions for other poets whom they thought would be worthy additions. At the time I was living in Racine, Wisconsin, an Easterner displaced by the academic job market to the Midwest. That evening in the summer of 1999 I thought it might be my parents calling after dinner, or maybe an old neighborhood friend. It was Leo Connellan, happy to discuss the possibilities for poems to include and glad to offer an array of suggestions for poets he believed ought to be considered, especially those who were not yet widely known and who therefore might slip under my radar. I had mailed well over fifty requests, and already received many helpful responses, but with the exception of friends I knew already he was the only poet who called me at home about the project, unabashed, enthusiastic, as though we shared something more than an impersonal call for submissions. He asked about my work, about my origins, spoke of his earlier life working in New York, carousing with Delmore Schwartz, Dylan Thomas, his present heart condition. Within minutes it was as though an ancient mariner in the art of poetry and the poetry world had somehow gotten my number—I could not choose but hear.

That evening on the telephone, and the several subsequent evenings when he called over the course of the year before his death, it became clear that Leo was never at a loss for impassioned speech or vivid anecdote. His best poems embody the same virtues, along with a penchant for surprising description and an embracing awareness of place and history. Here is the beginning of "York, Maine":

> Through the Cutty Sark motel room 21 picture window now
> the gray waves coming into York Beach like
> an invasion of plows pushing snow. Tomorrow
> the sun will scratch its chin and bleed along the skyline
> but today everything is gray poached in a steam of fog.

There is something utterly right and at the same time utterly strange about this description of York Beach, which is why Connellan's use of simile and metaphor here is so fresh, so surprising, despite being drawn from ordinary life—evidence of his honesty, his hard-won perception of reality. Unlike many poems content to stay in the moment, content to record the surfaces, "York, Maine" plows back through the genealogical history of place and finally to the poet's metaphysical preoccupations running just below the surface of the physical conditions of place and time, what he calls later in the poem "the under colors":

If I could find it, I could find the answer to life
to what to expect. God's energy, the day's changes,
clouds like a veil and then the sky clear blue
as if this world has no other color, the sea
just exploding here.

So many of Leo Connellan's poems situate themselves and the reader in motels, in liminal places where the poet's eye comes to regard both the ephemera of life passing and at the same time records the poet's own deeper longing for something more permanent. There is nothing dreamy about his regard, however, no Norman Rockwell sanctimony. More often than not one finds the hard edge of experience and equal parts compassion for the disenfranchised, and anger against a society that permits such injustice. Blue collar laborers, immigrants, the homeless—outsiders of all kinds—populate Leo Connellan's poems. He writes about skinheads, subway shooters, assassins, Cochise, Maine fishermen, the dolphin caught in the tuna net. Connellan's poems always turn toward the forgotten, toward the lost, and sometimes take on those marginal voices with unflinching truthfulness: "We was coming in from catching / scallops of violent water, the sea sucking / us under, boat sinking with Port in sight / so we all had to jump," begins his poem, "Fish," with perfect vocal pitch for its subject.

Among these lost for Leo Connellan are the artists, the poets made outcast by their own refusal to live according to the hypocrisies of the world in which they find themselves. His poems to Emily Dickinson, to Delmore Schwartz, to Federico Garcia Lorca, and to Oscar Wilde are vivid evocations of the imaginative life maintained in the face of social and artistic rejection, evocations that hold in common an impassioned counsel for courage in spite of apparent defeat. There is something unstinting in his gaze toward the world and in particular its defeated, and he turns that gaze on his own Irish American inheritance in his book-length poem, *The Clear Blue Lobster-Water Country*, that uses an at once head-long and recursive narrative to examine the fictionalized speaker's connection to a dominant male ancestor. In Connellan's poem, however, the pattern of repetition that is also the speaker's social and cultural inheritance reveals itself to be inextricable from the "ineluctable modalities" of history, in particular immigrant history:

> ... Oh many an Irish immigrant youth
> cursed by Saint Patrick myth and
> stupidity, foolish pride bragging how
>
> they were able to succeed enough to spare
> their children what they had to do, and in
> doing this, making many Irish American youth
>
> as crippled as he is back home in
> in rough green Irish Sea country.... (141)

In contrast to the sentimentalized version of Ireland, Connellan sees Catholic Ireland governed by guilt and repression, a pattern that is repeated in the new world. The "rough green Irish Sea country" is ruthlessly demythologized to become the source of grief in Irish immigrant Maine, the mythic-sounding name—the Clear Blue Lobster-Water Country—the antithesis of The Land of Youth in Irish lore. Instead, the ghosts of historical failure trail the fabled grandfather to the New World. "So ended American promise," he writes,

> in Michael The O'Dock... so ended the chance taking, the
> beautiful riskers that are the greatness of a country,
> ended the functioning that must come from
>
> inside us in each and everyone one of us, promise
> gone as much to the bottle here in America
> as any Irish farmer with Ireland,
>
> green Ireland, violent Ireland grape in its yearning
> Ireland always green in his eyes but alcohol
> his early death with all the old boys crying
>
> for The O'Dock who sailed away, his hand clutched
> in his mother's forever from Ireland, Eire
> of my soul my flesh wanders the earth... (142)

The Clear Blue Lobster-Water Country is Connellan's version of Kavanagh's "The Great Hunger," an epic recounting of social and moral and, finally, imaginative degradation. Michael The O'Dock, the inverse of Wallace Steven's The MacCullough and his archetype for imaginative humanity, breeds impotence in his son Big Billy and also in his grandson, Young Billy. The social inheritance the poem envisions is destructive and, as such, in a tone reminiscent of Berryman's Henry in *Dream Songs* (that other Irish American epic of the psyche), Connellan's fictive voice declares:

> We are a damned breed, the Irish. Young Billy gave
> his whole identity to Big Billy just to try
> to have his love...
>
> destruction of ourselves by ourselves
> until we are all forgotten
> dead among the dead...

At the same time, his embrace of other cultural traditions, namely Jazz, provides a model both for his own poems and for a vision of artistry that while absolutely honest in its rendering of defeat, nonetheless provides hope of transfiguration through art:

> Real horn men risk, when everyone's
> playing loud, fast, covering, Miles Davis
> blowing slow found us where
> we were lost and brings us back.

To risk in the art, to bring back the forgotten, even the dead, are the two great underlying motivations for Leo Connellan's poetry, and two reasons why we should go on reading him. Certainly we will be less alone, and more with each other and the rest of life, when we go to his work, when we hear from him.

Several months before his death, I read from my own poems at the University of Connecticut and, in what would turn out to be the one opportunity to sit down with Leo Connellan, missed him. We spoke on the phone again, however, and agreed that we would not miss the next opportunity. It was the last. I learned of his death by seeing his name on a list of the recently deceased in *Poets and Writers*. What could be more impersonal? Still, talking with Leo Connellan that first night over three years ago, I came to understand that for Leo there was nothing impersonal about poetry or the business of poetry, certainly nothing self-important, nothing that should impede the generous exchange of who we are with each other—that unmistakable and irreplaceable mark of our best character, our most human selves. Poetry for Leo Connellan was impassioned speech, captivating talk that sometimes invites us to listen and sometimes demands our attention in spite of ourselves, and to him, being a poet makes one a member of a tribe, a community of shared spirits, despite all the petty backbiting and jockeying for reputation that can obscure the better angels of the art. He once called that community, with appropriate largesse, "the heart's inner mix of brotherhood." In the face of the world's intransigence and injustice and our own flawed natures it is this inner depth of connection that his poetry most sought to reveal. And it is, as he observed in a poem, worth this life.

from *Northport Journal*, May 12 2004

Crossing America CD Puts Leo Connellan to Music

George Wallace

A rare CD of the late poet Leo Connellan reading all 30 sections of *Crossing America*—and with each of the sections provided a musical interpretation—was released earlier this year by Skuntry.com, a Wayne NJ record producer and is available on line. Verdict? To be concise, the CD is a show stopper. It is a work of great force and power that grows in likeability with each hearing.

Created by an intrepid group of producers who were both lucky and industrious, the CD brings to dramatic life the work of a poet who, for all his awards and recognitions, has not yet achieved the renown his work ought to command.

Leo Connellan (1928-2001), originally from Portland Maine, was poet laureate of Connecticut, was awarded the Shelley Memorial Award from the PSA (for the 1982 *Clear Blue Lobster-Water Country*), and was a writer who was praised by both the Bohemians and the Academic during his lifetime. In fact Connellan regularly won the praise of such established figures as Karl Shapiro, Richard Eberhart, Hayden Carruth, Anthony Hecht and Richard Wilbur.

Yet in his career he remained very much an outsider—perhaps because Connellan is a writer whose stance straddles worlds, one of those whose gift is both gruff as the earth and yet schooled by the grim unyielding demands of the intellect.

Now, with a CD of his work which has been released and is circulating in the New York area—through Skuntry.com at PO Box 4308 Wayne NJ 07474; info @skunty.com—the possibility emerges that a new public will be exposed to the work of a man who portrayed vividly the honest and passionate, the stalked and the helpless underbelly of America.

Connellan, declared Paragon House when they published his collected poems in 1989, "belongs squarely among Whitman's landscape of roving energy and spirit." Richard Wilbur called his poetry "vivid, harsh, spare, surely cadenced and colloquially eloquent." They both missed a key word—monumental: *Crossing America*, published in 1976, has a monumental quality to it.

It belongs in the category of the memorable writing of the twentieth century which is Whitmanian, in fact, mixing into its fundamental elegiac adoration of America's expanse a social and psychological consciousness missing in 19th century diction. To go along with Walt's incredible sense of celebration, here is alienation, protest and a profound sense of loss or failure in the shadow of America's literary tramps hoofing it across the continent.

James Dickey tries in his poem, "Folksinger of the Thirties," but against Connellan's work Dickey's pales—as hypothetical and distant compared to *Crossing America*, which thoroughly convinces us that he's lived the tale he's telling.

It also surpasses, one might argue easily, Bukowski. This is poetry that is far more than a pose, entertaining and authentic as Bukowski's beer-soaked musings may be. No less a critical authority than the H*udson Review* affirms this view, saying without compunction that Connellan writes "much better than Charles Bukowski, but with the same unrelenting fierceness, fueled by what he has seen of this country's underside."

This is nowhere more evident than in *Crossing America*, written in America's bicentennial year, seemingly with an acute consciousness of that fact.

Crossing America is quite simply an astounding work, a pastiche of snapshots and vignettes told in thirty sections. This long poem, dedicated to "the woman who crossed America with me" by Connellan, stands shoulder to shoulder with the great works of mid-20th century American story-tellers—Woody Guthrie, Jack Kerouac, Joe Kalar and John Steinbeck—if only for its scope, richness and trans-continental sweep.

We are confronted by the freezing shotgun moments on abandoned roads, suspicious and dangerous encounters in one-room backwash shacks.

Connellan plums the miserable depths of cold and loneliness, mercy and desperation, innocence and devotion, and even love, in section after section—as in Minook Illinois:

> Minook Illinois,
> one street out of no where through cornstocks.
> winter clutched the cornfields into Chicago.
> Cold, we couldn't get in out of the cold.
>
> But a lonely filling station owner risked
> letting his death in out of the night.
> I lay on his gas station floor and let her
> use me as a bed.
>
> I will never forget the cold into
> my kidneys or lying awake bearing the
> pain while she slept like a two month
> old child on the hill of its mother's tit.
>
> It was on that stone floor
> that I knew I loved her

It is composed of a myriad of rich small town American vignettes from a lost time when sheriffs ran drifters out of town, work gangs worked the apple country and cross-country hustlers whisked loose dollar bills from drunks in unwary midwestern bars. Appropriate to the time of its publication, during the nation's bicentennial, there is a harkening to a lost American wildness:

You are gone like buffalo never
existed in my time, except up from Pueblo,
Colorado, freak herd for truck diner
steaks now. In a museum for children
who will never know they roamed
open plains as you whistled on a halo
of congealed smoke through quiet
back-o-towns pulling our nation together
like a stubborn zipper.

The work is also infused with literary allusion, frequently direct, and directed toward poetic icons—Whitman, Lorca, Frost, Hart Crane. Sometime the reference leads Connellan to the elegiac, even in his hard-bitten weighed down New England overcoat twang, as in the brilliant section III on Vermont: "Frost lived in blood spouting green/ and white blinding snow and was/ stronger than anything that could/ kill him, but finally death yanking him out/ of the world he would never have left."

But the poet is also capable of crying out against social malaise. "Federico! we must not/ mark our Bicentennial/ until no man can languish// or die imprisoned in a land/ of the free and the brave" he writes, addressing Lorca, "you and I are bitter together." Or here, in Section XI: "Walt Whitman, because our whole song/ springs from the nest of your whiskers, I/ scream to you of poor people..." Connellan goes on to chastise poets from Allen Ginsberg to Gertrude Stein and Hart Crane for not noticing as poverty rotted through the body of the American people ("Allen Ginsberg, what on earth is Gertrude Stein/ doing to you down in your Cherry Valley...// Hart Crane, while you were noting the telephone poles stretching across our ghost...")

Time and again Connellan proves himself to have a voice possessed with the pungency of sourdough bread, haunted by experience—arresting as skunk cabbage in a new spring hollow. He hovers between presenting himself as a lost drifting son, an egregious hustler fleecing women and drunks, and an alter ego of the lost generation of working men set awash across hobo America during the Depression era. "*The apple country when/ Sunday smelled of our taste buds,/ our loneliness rattled in freight...*"

It should also be noted that there is frequently in the work a barely restrained power and unmasked wrath at the domineering behavior of fathers anywhere.

For all the years unable to cope I
write this, for all the ruined children
of others pacing their lives out in white
rooms I write this, stab me with thorns
of roses for writing this, let ground glass
be in all I eat for the loathsome back handed
ingrate treachery of writing this, but youth
does not dust its trail in the whim of the old man.

One might argue that a work with qualities like these deserves to be examined as one of the 20 major achievements of American poetry in the second half of the twentieth century. And one might hope that the newly released CD could prompt such a reexamination.

The story of how the CD came to pass makes for compelling reading in itself. It seems Leo met a group of musicians in Connecticut from a local arts collective called Hoobellatoo, who heard him read a poem in his 'skid-row lobsterman's twang' and were smitten.

That moment occurred in Willimantic, Connecticut, in the basement of Curbstone Press, recording some local poets, notes Chris King of Skuntry, when Leo departed from the scripted session during a break and read from a portion of *Crossing America*. It was brutal, frank and lyrical, and King and others were stunned.

Michael Shannon Friedman of Skuntry.com was later to call the poem a work which "considers America itself as a kind of poem, a desolate hymn to beauty, pain and loss...a testimony to the possibilities of encounter" with the road. Of Connellan's poetic oeuvre, he aptly notes its "disenfranchised, too-emotionally candid" nature, "not talk-show enough for the culture of victimization and complaint."

The poem reflects on Connellan's 1950s jaunts hitch hiking across America.

We hitchhiked America. I
still think of her.

I walk the old streets thinking I
see her, but never.

New buildings have gone up.
The bartenders who poured roses
into our glasses are gone.
We are erased.

Thankfully, notes King, the mike was not off, and for the rest of that field recording journey he and his friends "wore out a cassette dub of Leo's reading." It wasn't until later that King learned that what they had heard was only one section of the thirty-section epic, and were able to get Connellan to record the entire work.

After recording Connellan reading the poem in its entirety, King and friends reckoned that the material amounted to 37 minutes, it turned out, and after living inside the poem for awhile, determined to coax a range of musicians to work up musical interpretations for each section.

That effort brought them on a pilgrimage to locations around the nation as diverse as Brooklyn and New Jersey to Vermont, Maine and rural Illinois. They recorded Matt Fuller in a garage in Los Angles, William Teague on the South Side of St Louis, an anonymous tuba player at an herb store and a brass band at a high school. "We crossed America with Leo's poem," said King.

The result is compilation of a panoply of music, as varied and diverse as America. There's the plaintive, front-porch harmonica work of Pops Farmer (and Rich Hubbs' backwoods banjo). There are shattered modernist pianistic moments, courtesy of Nate Shaw. Moody trumpet and bass work come from the artistry of the Esser Brothers. Dave Stone Trio's incredibly driving be-bop sax racing through passages.

Quite a few of the strongest pieces carry a mountain-home rangy angularity to them, as written and performed by Three Fried Men, including the sections on Green Vermont, True With Silence, and Just Around The Corner From Night. This group offers up a funky roadhouse sound, three wheels on the ground, some crazy combination of Lowell George, Tom Waits and Zappa, authentic and tangential as a hobbling and hungover country drunk.

And a clear highlight of the CD is the chain gang thrust of The Apple Country, performed by Rosco Gordon & The Rotton Dogs.

Leo the Ventriloquist

William Collins Watterson

Leo Connellan's literary sensibility is essentially elegiac but his poetry strives alternately for refinement and rawness. In the meditative, lyrical vein he speaks in his own voice, but in the primitivistic (i.e." pastoral") vein he affects the speech of the unlettered (street people, down-and-outers and, if the poems are set in Maine, farmers and fishermen with Downeast accents and idioms). Some of the latter poems are mono-vocal persona poems ("Lobster Fisherman." "Fish," "The $100 Street Person," "Shooter," "Lobster Claw") while others are persona poems which also include fragments of interpolated dialogue ("In Lobster Night," "Edwin Coombs," " Amelia, Mrs. Brooks of My Old Childhood," "Unsafe Survivor," "The Clear Blue Lobster-Water Country"). Although Connellan's poems return repeatedly to the themes of poverty, sexual abuse, violent and/or premature death, urban alienation, alcoholism, nostalgia for childhood, and his Irish ancestry, it is the poems with voices from the underclasses which are responsible for the pigeon-holing of Connellan as a populist writer. Hailed by Hayden Carruth as "the poet of the American working class" foregrounding "working-class values as the nucleus of his program," Connellan is characterized by Richard Eberhart as outside "the mainstream of university poetry for university-educated readers." The latter holds that because Connellan's "textbook is raw life" his "words can be understood by anyone." Such generosity, if that is the right word, seems calculatedly evasive; it passes off socio-political commentary as aesthetic insight and/or artistic achievement.

Although the vast majority of Connellan's poems, whether lyric or narrative, are written in the first-person (which I take to be the autobiographical voice of the poet waxing meditative and struggling, as all true poets do and must, with language and form), I wish to focus here on the primitive voices which Connellan interpolates into his poems.

His ventriloquism works fine at the level of local color ("No-o, Amelyuh duzzent live withus.... No-o, Amelyuh's across th'bridge t'Brewer") is a credible stab at "Downeast" patois, but it gets him into trouble when the "thrown" voice is inconsistent. Consider the speaker of "Lobster Claw," an aging lobsterman in Rockland, Maine who exclaims: "I am not easily caught, but overwhelming fatigue is my nemesis." As semanticists have taught us, connotative meaning consists, among other things, of levels of abstraction, formality, and intensity in word choice, with the first two as hallmarks of written rather than spoken prose. We hear Connellan the poet in this formulation, not the voice of a fisherman. A few lines later the same voice will say "but Potato fellas can hit too, that's the fun of it," though the capitalizing of the letter "P" is also obviously a literary device which can't be rendered orally. Likewise in "Fish," a rough and ready veteran of the seas is paradoxically ungrammatical and prissily discriminating in a prosaic fashion: "They come on the boat and rob us" modulates to "Sun up we'll be out scalloping, slices of salt water shaving our faces erotic in the sea's slap, what a groin ache! But the joy of this life is gone. It used to be wonderful, the nicest part of our fishing was returning." In "Lobster Fisherman" the diction also sounds written. The old salt's "It's May-n-we gut th'lobster fever again" devolves into the formality and abstraction of expository prose which the colloquialisms can't conceal: "Now anyone-n-everyone with instruments that register depth and ocean floor, technology takin' too much until now th' thrill for doin' hit in wind sea salt sand anticipation vanish." One could trace the same inconsistency of tone in the voices of some of Connellan's urban street people, though in all fairness the fact that he limited his ventriloquism to fewer than twenty poems suggests that the poet may himself have been aware of the problems attendant on it and abandoned the practice.

Richard Wilbur has labeled Connellan as the poet of the "poor, the unlucky, the disesteemed" and spoken of his "credible compassion for (and identification with)" such people. I would add that Connellan achieves that vision for the most part in poems of skilful diction in which he—the poet—is talking in his own voice, a voice which often affects rawness but which is usually tonally consistent. These poems are about misfortunes in contemporary life and the reader is at home in them. When Connellan essays primitivism, however, and his fishermen talk poetic prose peppered with Downeast-isms, we find ourselves squarely in the realm of the pastoral. There artifice calls attention to itself and the poet is alienated from his own discourse, dispossessed as a shepherd in a Virgilian eclogue and banished from the innocence—and spontaneity—of an arcadia which he sought to salvage.

from *Negative Capability*, 1994

Leo and Sam

Richard White

"He is a tremendous companion."

So Edmund Burke said of Samuel Johnson. It can be said, too, of Leo Connellan. Indeed, the parallels between the English lexicographer and the Irish-American poet are stunning. Their differences are readily summed up.

Johnson was, of course, a classicist, a Tory, an Anglican, a monarchist, and a firm believer in the caste system that so effectively excluded him from the first table. Connellan is none of these. But—both were a source of anxiety to their elders; both left the university without a degree; both battled poverty, fear and loneliness in a terrific struggle—and a long one—to stake their claim in a literary world dominated by the privileged, and beset on all sides by stragglers, tricksters, and fakes.

Both knew firsthand the underside of life in a great city. Johnson's Grub Street years, when he was often hungry, sometimes homeless, brought him into daily association with the bohemians, the criminal, the vicious, and the lost. Connellan's foray into New York provided him with a similar education. With scant resources, and with even less encouragement, both learned to survive, and both were left with an abiding compassion for the poor, the sick, the outcast and the defeated.

Even in the meager years, Johnson would thrust coins into the fists of waifs asleep in doorways. When he had a home, he made room for a contrary collection of strays, and supported them even when their bickering threatened to drive him into the street. Connellan is a notoriously soft touch who has often kept failing families afloat when his own funds were perilously low.

Both loved cats. Connellan maintains a herd of ten. Johnson would go out himself to buy oysters for "Hodge," because he feared that his faithful servant, Frank Barber, might come to resent the cat if he were asked to run that errand.

Both were profoundly devoted to the women they married. "Tetsy" Porter-florid, affected, a figure of fun to David Garrick and his set-believed in Johnson. She risked—and lost—her legacy in helping him to make a start in life. She was, in many ways, a trial, and Johnson adored her.

Nancy Connellan believed in her man. She shelved her own ambitions, and she worked long days in a draining job to give him time to write. She gave him their only child. To this day, he gives her first priority and his absolute, unwavering loyalty and love.

Johnson and Connellan were cast on the grand scale, men of gargantuan mold-and of like appetite. Boswell expressed disgust at Johnson's approach to the table. Boswell, of course, never missed a meal in his life. Connellan, too, is a trencherman of note. When one has slept under bridges, sold his blood to make the rent, and resorted to a dozen different makeshift strategies to get through another day, food is an object of downright devotion.

The grape, too, had its role to play in the lives of both writers. Johnson said he "used to slink home" when he was in his cups. Connellan said two breweries and a distillery went bust when he gave up the stuff. And both authors quit cold.

Neither could be called a slave to fashion, Until Johnson was taken up by the Thrales, his appearance was well to the left of couth.... "As for clean linen," he said, "I have no passion for it." Connellan, while decidedly on the side of the hygienic, favors the Unmade Bed School of Sartorial Options. He once had four suits, but then he gave up pinochle.

Both writers acquired a strong social sense, reflected in a range of acquaintance that covers the full spectrum of humanity.

Talk is their common passion. Johnson, late in life, virtually abandoned ink. Conversation became his medium—if it can be called conversing when one speaker so predominates over the rest. Johnson had the advantage of a voice that could have carried across the border in Wales. He was also, conveniently, a bit deaf, so if another tried to enter the flow of talk he was likely to be run over, unnoticed, unheard and unlamented. Connellan himself does not whisper, and his flow of talk is riparian. Like Johnson, Connellan will wait warily till a topic is started, then he wades in and takes no prisoners.

The talk of both men reverberates with opinion, crackles with wit, and delights the auditor with the novelty of image and the audacity of the humor. Their talk reflects an aggressive stance in confrontation with life. As Boswell would have it, they "talk for victory." Combat is their element. Having fought their way to the fore against tremendous odds, neither is inclined to check his weapons at the door. And yet none could be more sensitive, nor more sincerely apologetic, should offense be taken.

But should offense be given, the offender cannot hope to escape unscathed. Johnson, when a usurper glommed onto his chair in the wings of a playhouse, politely requested the return of his seat. When the oaf refused, Johnson tossed him—and the chair—into the pit. He kayoed the odious Thomas Osborne with a folio Greek testament for calling him a liar. And his letter to Lord Chesterfield is the literary equivalent of a right cross—delivered by the late Mr. Joseph Louis.

Connellan was obliged to scrap his way out of encounters with sociopaths in the City, and during his youthful wandering through 44 states. He still bears the scar of a close encounter with an aspiring axe-murderer. And once he chucked out a dainty gentleman critic from a Very Important Newspaper who sniffed at the clutter and dust that ornamented the poet's den.

Rarest, perhaps, among traits these two giants have in common is their generosity to other writers. Indeed, the notion that one writer would actually help another borders on the bizarre. Yet it was Johnson who saved the exasperating Oliver Goldsmith from debtors' prison by negotiating the sale of *The Vicar of Wakefield*. And Johnson's surgical ministrations to the poems, essays, plays and novels of others can never be accurately told. He hated being asked to look at others' work, but he would do it, and he would improve the work significantly. And he would often find a place for it. Ask any struggling writer to set a value on that.

Connellan has helped any number of poets to get published, and he is responsible for getting the work of at least three novelists—including this one—into print. And this he has done while engaged clear up to his eyelashes in his own ongoing battle for the recognition, the honors, the respect that he and his work so richly merit.

Samuel Johnson and Leo Connellan, two titans of totally different places and times, loom large in this poor inkslinger's private Valhalla. Nothing about them is small—not their talent, not their persons, not their courage, nor their respective bodies of work. But even those Herculean dimensions are dwarfed by their prodigious largeness of heart.

Some Words About Leo

Richard Wilbur

Leo Connellan was a remarkable poet, as I knew from the first things he ever showed me. He wrote mostly about himself, and the particulars of his life, but with a driven honesty that universalized his poems. He had the ability to build a digressive narrative, or a circling, obsessive meditation, without losing impetus. There was power and an inescapable rhythm in his jagged lines. He insisted on being a poet in spite of a life that was often hard, emotionally and practically. I hand it to him.

"By the Blue Sea": The Art of Leo Connellan

Baron Wormser

A month or so after Leo Connellan's death, I gave a talk about him and I read aloud a number of his poems. Although I had read Leo's poems many times, I realized I had never read them to an audience.

It was, for me, a powerful and illuminating experience. I read some of the longer ones such as "By the Blue Sea" and I found myself experiencing a sort of energy that only comes from a certain sort of poetic power. For lack of a better word, I would call it "Whitmanesque," in deference to the poet who is, in America at least, a great source of such energy. It is an energy that accrues over pages and that is declamatory. It points at things; it scrutinizes; it names; it invokes past experiences; it turns the experience over as if it were an object and looks at it from other angles. It is a moving highway and like a highway it is as much about the journey as the end. The shaping, controlling energies that are manifest in formalist poetry don't feel so crucial in poetry such as Leo's. That isn't, I rush to say, on account of a lack of art on Leo's part—far from it (as I hope to make clear). It's rather that such poetry is open-ended in the sense that it is trying to encompass an experience rather than define it. It seeks to know what it is like to be someone else or one's own self and its way of doing that is by reconnoitering. The highway isn't a straight interstate. It has curves and stops. One feels how the poet may be at moments baffled by what the poet confronts. Yet the poet moves forward.

I'd like to look at how a poem such as "By the Blue Sea" is put together. The poem, like many of Leo's best poems (to my mind) is about the lives of women and men. I think Leo Connellan was one of the most honest poets who ever wrote about the relations between women and men. Poets are fond of singing the praises of love but Leo preferred to sing about the wages of love—how it goes bad, how it pretends to be something other than what it is, how it masks lust and indifference and cruelty, how it turns so easily to regret, how it festers and confuses, how it becomes another lever to pull to get what you want. And, perhaps most remarkably, Leo considered the woman's point of view as a value in its own right. That seems obvious to us in what Leo called "this / liberated 'Ms.' feminist / time," but I wonder how many men have written as many poems as Leo wrote that presented a woman's side of a story and neither sugarcoated nor exaggerated what a woman might go through with a man.

In "By the Blue Sea," Leo tells the story of a woman in coastal Maine who is loved by a young man and who loves him back but who marries another man, a hard working and brutal fisherman. Eventually she leaves this man (after bearing him five sons) and remarries but that husband dies. At the poem's end she meets her first love again but it is all too late. Too much pain has occurred. There is no miraculous redemption. Her struggle to be her own woman has been her struggle and that is all that can be said. It is something very substantial to say.

The way poets tell stories is not, of course, the way fiction writers tell stories. Poetry is a leaping art; those white spaces between stanzas can be gulfs of any duration the poet chooses. Leo was very adroit at constructing narratives that covered, in effect, decades. One device he favored and used to great effect in "By the Blue Sea" is what I would call buried incantation. That is to say, he would repeat a phrase over and over throughout a poem. The phrase was a descriptive tag but also took on a life of its own. It could be a simple phrase such as "blue sea," that appears in the second stanza of the poem—"who took her by the blue sea"—and in the penultimate line of the poem—"the blue sea frosting...." It could be a phrase that is varied as in "Slowly she walked by..." and then much later in the poem "who used to / walk slowly in front of the / house..." It could be a sort of charm, a phrase one repeats again and again to summarize a situation as in "a man / who had the same job the / the father of the boy she / wanted had...." What, as a whole, these repetitions do is to take a linear narrative and make it, as phrases keep recurring, more like a circle. They enshrine the active presence of the past in the poem's present moment.

Part of the genius of "By the Blue Sea" is that Leo constructs a point of view that isn't easy to pin down. The poem is told in third person and the man whom the woman loves so fervently at the beginning of the poem exists in the third person. Yet at one point in the poem an "I" breaks in to say "I hear the crying / children..." and most powerfully in the last line of the poem an "our" appears, implying what the reader may have felt all along: the man and the narrator are one. The third person distance the poem creates is all the more heartbreaking for its being a strangely artificial distance, as if the narrator were rehearsing something he had heard somewhere and was not implicated in emotionally.

Leo also favored the use of something like a chorus in many of his narrative poems. Social commentary and remarks are delivered in a direct, this-is-how-it-was tone. Sometimes these passages are indented from the margin that most of the poem follows, as in the fourth stanza of the poem where the narrator notes that the young man "had no job or money, he / wasn't supposed to be / doing what they were doing." Sometimes the chorus is brutally direct as in the stanza where the Fish Husband takes a new wife, "another woman to wipe / noses, clean and / cook for a flock...." Sometimes the chorus is simply a parenthetical, worldly-wise aside—"she married / (you have to eat)...." What these passages do is guide the poem through decades by imposing a fact that is also a tone—the world is always with us. Leo was very much a poet who was aware of how social realities conditioned human behaviors. There was very little lyrical forgetting of social identity in Leo's work. A highly moral poet, Leo was scandalized by poets who took lexical reality as the only one with which poets had to contend.

Leo's awareness of the social tyrannies gave him a voice that could be disarmingly folksy. In "By the Blue Sea" he uses transitions such as "Well, all this time..." and "Finally, she took..." and, again, "Well, she was a proud girl..." and "Now, another life later...." These aren't transitions I would recommend to beginning poets because they easily seem hackneyed. In Leo's hands they don't because he is very aware of how insinuating they are and how there is something awful in that quality. He wrote against glibness and he was aware of how easy it was to dispense with all the stubborn hurt of human experience in such phrases.

His using them testified to how committed he was to giving the world of approved social wisdom its terrible yet easy-going say.

In terms of what used to be called verse technique, Leo was masterful at splitting stanzas so that the reader never can be quite sure where and how a stanza is going to end. Most of the time in "By the Blue Sea" he uses the stanza as a narrative unit. That unit varies enormously in length, however. When it is shortened, we feel it viscerally as in the two-line stanza "And it was the usual / sorrow back and forth." Toward the end of the poem when the emotional consequences of the woman's actions and the man's actions mount up he breaks the stanzas to register the emotional pain. When he writes "now / one day the boy she loved all those years ago / by the blue sea...now" and then pauses in the void of white space before moving to the next stanza's "one day the boy..." the reader feels the grief of time in that hiatus between stanzas. One feels it all the more because the poem has moved along from stanza to stanza obeying the forward movement of life itself and then there is, as the poem moves to its conclusion, a feeling of the waste of the years that mocks that forwardness.

How a poet tells a story is also a matter of the particular word choices a poet makes. The words are actors in poems in a way that they aren't in prose stories; their physicality as sounds and the rhythms they create are entities in their own right. Their tones, as to how colloquial or formal they are, also matter a great deal. The words are tuned to all the other words and how concrete or abstract they are matters enormously.

There are many word choices in "By the Blue Sea" that jolt a reader. Some of the jolts come from the powerful, no-holds-barred physicality of Leo's language as in the beginning of the poem where love is "a spike in her wind pipe..." or the description of the smell of the fisherman husband: "cigar fish and gasoline like / the smell from first touch / of a match to fresh cigarette / making young children / car sick...." Leo never wrote for the squeamish.

Other word choices show careful shades about matters that at first glance don't seem to call for much discrimination. The fisherman is described as "a mean husband and / furious." The two adjectives have an almost sickening and certainly frightening power. That Leo put only one of the adjectives onto the noun and let the other one end the sentence by itself makes the man's anger all the more ominous. The husband encompasses the meanness, as it is attached to him, but the fury is something that exists in its own right.

At the same time, there are word choices that are heartbreaking. When the drunken lover meets the woman outside the dance hall, the narrator notes that "still even then to her / he was still even then one / of those lovely people she had / hoped to marry into...." The repetition makes it plain that the narrator isn't making excuses for the man's drunkenness; he "staggered" up to her. Yet there is the word "lovely" in all its gracefulness and feeling. This combination of the rough and the tender isn't common in many poets' work. Typically they are on one side of the street or the other. Leo, however, was adept at showing how suffering and beauty can come to the same occasion.

Leo was a naturalist in the sense of being a writer who paid great attention to the actual circumstances of life. Yet at moments he was very free with language, as he gave metaphor its due. In the scene outside the dance hall he writes of the "singing leaves of lust." The strength of the poem's ending stems in part from showing how metaphor lives in people's minds: "She told him she / used to lie pregnant / fearing the babies / would come out with / three heads because / of what he and she / did by the pines...." The power of the imagination couldn't be stronger or more real. We sympathize with the Fish Woman.

That Leo capitalized such a name as if he were creating a mythic figure was very just. He was creating mythic figures. He was showing that such people were utterly defined by their circumstances and were more than their circumstances. He was showing that their actions were determined and yet could be free. He was showing the mocking awfulness of definition, of how words stick to a person as much as those smells of cigar and fish and gasoline. Yet he was bestowing a sort of grandeur on a life that wasn't very grand at all, that was both hard and confining.

The contemporary world adores glamour and that trait was never what Leo Connellan was about. As it is a superficial thing glamour fades but the emotional reality that Leo conveyed in his best poems and the art that went into creating that reality seem to me to an achievement that won't fade. Recently, when I read "By the Blue Sea" to a group of teachers, there was dead silence after the poem. Finally, one woman raised her hand and said in a tight, aching voice, "Who is that poet? I need to know. I need to have that book." Leo, I think, would have understood the moment very well.

Contributors

Mary and John Abbott retired to New York City in 2003. Mary Abbott taught English at Windham High School for 25 years. John Abbott retired as Professor and Head of English at the University of Connecticut where he taught for 39 years.

David B. Axelrod's latest of nineteen books is *How to Apologize*. He published in hundreds of magazines and in a fourteen languages.
Find him at his websites: http://writersunlimited.org/laureate,
http://poetrydoctor.org, and http://poetrydoctor.org.
His email is: axelrodthepoet@yahoo.com

David Bradt has published stories, essays, translations and interviews, along with the usual kinds of academic writing. His interviews include talks with novelists, poets, historians, and playwrights. His conversations with May Sarton and John Irving for New Hampshire Public Television have been syndicated nationwide. He is Emeritus Professor of English at Southern New Hampshire University.

Harry Brody was awarded a Bread Loaf fellowship for *Fields* (Ion Books, Memphis, 1987), and his poems still pop up occasionally in the magazines. A death-row lawyer, he lives in Sarasota, Florida.

Gary Carlson has taught at Norwalk Community College since 1997. In the fall of 2000, he originated the annual CT Writers' Conference at NCC. He organized and hosts NCC's very successful film series. His fiction and nonfiction have appeared in *The Connecticut Review, The Apalachee Quarterly, The Vermont Literary Review, Curious Rooms, DISCoveries Magazine, The Hartford Courant, The Fairfield Weekly,* and *The New Haven Register*. Carlson lives in West Haven, along with his beagle Jessie. In his spare time he follows baseball and collects music; he is an avid gardener and also enjoys motorcycling, kayaking, and hiking.

Bill Carpenter grew up in Waterville and returned to Maine to help start the College of the Atlantic, where he still teaches. His latest novel is *The Wooden Nickel* (Little, Brown, 2002), whose epigraph is taken from Leo's "By the Blue Sea."

Hayden Carruth published more than thirty books, chiefly of poetry, but also a novel, four books of criticism, and two anthologies. Recent books included *Doctor Jazz: Poems 1996-2000* (2001), and *Toward the Distant Islands: New and Selected Poems* (Copper Canyon Press, 2006) He received the Lenore Marshall Award, the Paterson Poetry Prize, he Ruth Lilly Prize, among many others. Carruth lived in Vermont for many years before residing in Munnsville, New York, with his wife, the poet Joe-Anne McLaughlin Carruth. He died in 2008.

William J. Cibes, Jr. is Chancellor Emeritus of the Connecticut State University System, which he served during Leo Connellan's tenure as Poet-in-Residence at CSU. He was formerly Secretary of the Office of Policy and Management in the administration of Governor Lowell Weicker, following his service as Representative for the 39th District in the Connecticut General Assembly. He earned a Ph.D. in Politics from Princeton University, and was Professor of Government at Connecticut College.

James Coleman is a retired college teacher living in Norwich, Connecticut. He received an N.E.A. Fellowship in Writing in 1977, and was named a Distinguished Advocate for the Arts by the State of Connecticut in 2001. Leo Connellan was a frequent visitor to his classes.

Amy Connellan graduated from Eastern Connecticut State University in 1993 with a B.A. in history. She is the daughter of Leo Connellan and lives in Shoreham, Vermont.

Nancy A. Connellan graduated in 1956 from the University of California at Berkeley with a B.A. in English. She is the widow of Leo Connellan and lives in Shoreham, Vermont. Amy and Nancy Connellan share their home with a dog and a cat.

Christopher Corbett, a Maine-born writer, worked as a journalist for 20 years, primarily with The Associated Press. He is the author of *Vacationland,* a novel published by Viking/Penguin and *Orphans Preferred: The Twisted Truth and Lasting Legacy of the Pony Express*, published by Broadway Books, a division of Random House. He next book—*The Poker Bride: A Story of the Chinese in the American Goldfields* will be published in early 2010 by Grove/Atlantic Monthly. He teaches journalism at the University of Maryland-Baltimore County.

Robert Creeley was an originator of the "Black Mountain" school of poetry. He wrote more than 60 books of poetry and criticism He was a member of the University of Buffalo faculty from 1966 to 2003 when he left to become a Distinguished Professor at Brown University. He received many major honors and distinctions including the Bollingen Prize, the Lila Wallace/Reader's Digest Writers Award, and the Lannan Lifetime Achievement Award. He was elected a Chancellor of the Academy of American Poets in 1999. He died in 2005.

G. Scott Deshefy, poet and behavioral-ecologist, lives in eastern Connecticut with his wife (Nancy), daughter (Alea), Belgium sheep dog, Shadow, and a large clowder of cats. His poetry, essays and scientific papers have appeared in a variety of literary magazines and academic journals. In addition to editing the Earth Day poetry anthology, *Touch the Earth*, in 1992, Scott has written two books of selected poems: *Houyhnhnms All* (1998) and *Shadow Stones* (2003). Scott was the first Green Party candidate to run for US Congress as Representative of Eastern Connecticut 2008.

Franz Douskey knew Leo Connellan from the 1970's, when they were both published by New Quarto Editions. Their friendship flourished during the El Bardo The Legend years with the loyal friendship and support of Andy Thibault, Douskey's favorite anarchist. Franz Douskey has published several books of poetry, including one from Arizona State University and another from University of Georgia. His writing has appeared in hundreds of publications, including *The New Yorker, The Nation, Yankee, Rolling Stone, Las Vegas Life, Down East, Cavalier, Baseball Diamonds* (Doubleday & Co.) and INK.

Christopher Fahy is the author of *Limerock: Maine Stories* and 14 other books, among them the novels *Fever 42, Breaking Point* and *Chasing the Sun*, which was inspired by Leo Connellan. He lives in Thomaston, Maine.

Emily Grosholz's fourth book of poetry, *The Abacus of Years*, appeared in 2002 from David R. Godine. She has published many critical essays and reviews, most often in *The Hudson Review* where she serves as advisory editor. She teaches philosophy at the Pennsylvania State University.

Constance Hunting taught creative writing at the University of Maine where she was a full professor. *Natural Things: Collected Poems 1969-1998* was published by the National Poetry Foundation. She founded the Puckerbrush Press in 1971 and began publishing poetry and other work by aspiring young writers. Seven years later, she founded the *Puckerbrush Review*, a journal of poetry, essays, short fiction, and reviews, often by writers from Maine. She was the editor of *The Puckerbrush Review* and Puckerbrush Press until her death in 2006.

Sydney Lea founded and for thirteen years edited *New England Review*. He has published a novel, two collections of naturalist essays, and eight collections of poetry, with a ninth forthcoming. His new and selected poems, *To the Bone*, won the 1998 Poets' Prize, and his 2000 collection, *Pursuit of a WOUND*, was a finalist for the Pulitzer Prize. His most recent poetry volume is *GHOST PAIN* (Sarabande, 2005).

Sheila A. Murphy is a graduate of Albertus Magnus College, with an M.A. from Boston College and an M.A.L.S. from Wesleyan University. She taught English and Latin in Massachusetts, Hawaii, and Connecticut, grades seven through college, for 34 years. As a Teacher-Consultant for the Connecticut Writing Project at the University of Connecticut, she facilitated two teacher research projects and co-edited two collections of essays. She served as a field consultant for the National Council to Teachers of English poetry-writing textbook *Getting the Knack*. After retiring, she taught and supervised student teachers, and now teaches poetry and memoir writing to senior citizens. She has 4 children, 8 living grandchildren, and a Welsh corgi. She and her husband of fifty years live in Connecticut and Massachusetts. Her poems, celebrating the memory of her Irish ancestors and two grandchildren who died of Spinal Muscular Atrophy, have appeared in *Caduceus, The Litchfield Review, Long River Run, Peregrine*, and *Fields of Vision*. Her chapbook *View from a Kayak in Autumn* was published by The Argian Press in 2008.

Marilyn Nelson is the author or translator of twelve books and three chapbooks. Her book *The Homeplace* won the 1992 Annisfield-Wolf Award and was a finalist for the 1991 National Book Award. *The Fields Of Praise: New And Selected Poems* won the 1998 Poets' Prize and was a finalist for the 1997 National Book Award, the PEN Winship Award, and the Lenore Marshall Prize. *Carver: A Life In Poems* won the 2001 Boston Globe/Hornbook Award and the Flora Stieglitz Straus Award, was a finalist for the 2001 National Book Award, a Newbery Honor Book, and a Coretta Scott King Honor Book. *Fortune's Bones* was a Coretta Scott King Honor Book and won the Lion and the Unicorn Award for Excellence in North American Poetry. *A Wreath For Emmett Till* won the 2005 Boston Globe-Horn Book Award and was a 2006 Coretta Scott King Honor Book, a 2006 Michael L. Printz Honor Book, and a 2006 Lee Bennett Hopkins Poetry Award Honor Book. *The Cachoeira Tales And Other Poems* won the L.E. Phillabaum Award and was a finalist for the Los Angeles Times Book Award. Her honors include two NEA creative writing fellowships, the 1990 Connecticut Arts Award, an A.C.L.S. Contemplative Practices Fellowship, a Fulbright Teaching Fellowship, three honorary doctorates, and a fellowship from the J.S. Guggenheim Memorial Foundation. Nelson is a professor emerita of English at the University of Connecticut; founder and director of Soul Mountain Retreat, a small writers' colony; and the former (2001-2006) Poet Laureate of the State of Connecticut.

William Packard, poet, playwright, novelist, editor, and founder of *The New York Quarterly*, was the author of six volumes of poetry, and taught poetry and literature at NYU and other universities in New York. He was author of the textbooks *The Art of the Playwright*, *The Art of Screenwriting*, *The Poet's Dictionary*, and *The Art of Poetry Writing*. He died in 2002.

Tim Peeler's most recent books are *Checking Out* (poetry) from Hub City Press and *Voices from Baseball in Catawba County* (oral history) from Mint Hill Books. He lives in Hickory, North Carolina.

Sanford Phippen, who interviewed Leo Connellan on his *Maine PBS* series *A Good Read*, is the author of twelve books. He teaches in the English Department at the University of Maine and is the editor of the *Puckerbrush Review*.

Vivian Shipley is the Connecticut State University Distinguished Professor and the Editor of *Connecticut Review* from Southern Connecticut State University. Her seventh book of poems, *Hardboot: Poems New & Old*, (Southeastern Louisiana University Press, 2005) won the 2006 Paterson Prize for Sustained Literary Achievement and the 2006 Connecticut Press Club Prize for Best Creative Writing. She has also published five chapbooks. Shipley won the 2005 Lifetime Achievement Award for Service to the Literary Community from the Library of Congress Connecticut Center for the Book. *Gleanings: Old Poems, New Poems* (Southeastern Louisiana University Press, 2003) won the 2004 Paterson Prize for Sustained Literary Achievement. *When There is No Shore* won the 2003 Connecticut Book Award for Poetry from the Library of Congress Connecticut Center for the Book and the 2002 Word Press Poetry Prize. In 2007, she won the Hackney Literary Award for Poetry from Birmingham-Southern University in Alabama and the *New Millennium* Poetry Prize. In 2008, she was named the Faculty Scholar from Southern Connecticut State University for *Gleanings*. A new book of poetry, *All of Your Messages Have Been Erased*, is forthcoming in January, 2010 from Southeastern Louisiana University Press. She will be inducted to the University of Kentucky Hall of Fame for distinguished Alumni in April, 2010.

David A. Shippee is a graduate of Fairfield Preparatory School and Iona College. He spent 42 years in the personal insurance business, and is finally the graduate of a very lengthy, and detailed course of study of "THE WORLD ACCORDING TO LEO." This last course of learning took place over more than 18 years of nightly phone calls, infrequent eggs at Charlene's Diner in Jewett City, and countless scribbled notes to, and from, El Bardo Connellan. Seeing Leo named Poet Laureate of Connecticut was the crowning moment of all this intense training.

Wally Swist's most recent poems are scheduled to appear in *Alimentum: The Literature of Food, Appalachia, Lalitamba*, and the 30th Anniversary Issue of *Puckerbrush Review*. His books include *The New Life*, selected by Small Press Distribution as one of their top thirty bestselling books of poetry, and *Mount Toby Poems*, issued in a fine letterpress limited edition by Timberline Press in 2009. A short biographical documentary film regarding his work, *In Praise of the Earth*, was released by filmmaker Elizabeth Wilda through WildArts. A recording of a poem from his reading in the Sunken Garden Poetry Festival is archived at http://npr.org. He is a recipient of two Artist Fellowship Awards in Poetry from the Connecticut Commission on the Arts (1978 and 2003). The Edwin Mellen Press, of Lewiston, NY, issued his essay *High-pressure Weather and Country Air: The Friendship of Robert Frost and Robert Francis* as an academic monograph in 2009.

Andy Thibault, author of *Law & Justice In Everyday Life*, is an adjunct professor of Writing and a mentor in the MFA Writing Program at Western Connecticut State University in Danbury. He is a licensed private investigator, professional boxing judge and consulting editor for the literary journal *Connecticut Review*. He delivered the 2004 Pew Memorial Lecture In Journalism at Widener University, Chester, Pa. Thibault serves on the board of the Connecticut Center For The Book, an affiliate of the Library of Congress, and chairs a fund that has awarded more than $176,000 to young writers in Connecticut. Thibault blogs @ http://cooljustice.blogspot.com/ and can be reached by email @ tntcomm82@cs.com

Daniel Tobin is the author of four books of poems, *Where the World is Made*, co-winner of the 1998 Katherine Bakeless Nason Prize, *Double Life, The Narrows*, finalist for the Foreword Book Award in Poetry), and *Second Things*, as well as a book of criticism, *Passage to the Center: Imagination and the Sacred in the Poetry of Seamus Heaney*, and numerous essays on poetry. He has also edited *The Book of Irish American Poetry from the 18th Century to the Present, Light in Hand: The Selected*

Early Poems of Lola Ridge, and with Pimone Triplett *Poet's Work, Poet's Play: Essays on the Practice and the Art*. Among his awards are the "Discovery" / The Nation Award, The Robert Penn Warren Award, the Robert Frost Fellowship, as well as fellowships in poetry from the National Endowment for the Arts and the John Simon Guggenheim Foundation. Widely published in journals, his work has been anthologized in *The Bread Loaf Anthology of New American Poets, The Norton Introduction to Poetry, Hammer and Blaze*, among other collections, and has been featured on *Poetry Daily* and *Verse Daily*. He is presently Chair of the Department of Writing, Literature, and Publishing at Emerson College in Boston.

George Wallace, Suffolk County's First Poet Laureate, is an award winning poet and journalist from New York. He is co-host of *PoetryBrook*, a SUNY Stony Brook poetry radio show which is streamed live on the worldwide web at www.wusb.org Thursdays at 6 p.m. In 2000, he founded *Poetrybay*, a prestigious online poetry publication which was selected in 2004 by Stanford U. for archiving and distribution through the world-wide LOCKSS. His work has been translated into French, Spanish, Italian, German, Korean, Bengali, Russian and Macedonian. His concert dates include appearances with composer Leonard Lehrman and jazz composer David Amram—with whom he has collaborated on three CDs. Winner of the CW Post Poetry Prize, Wallace is a primary force behind numerous poetry journals, anthologies, reading series, radio and television poetry programs.

William Collins Watterson has been a member of the English Department at Bowdoin College since 1976, and is presently Edward Little Professor of English Language and Literature. He holds a Ph.D. from Brown University. His scholarly articles and essays have appeared in *Milton Quarterly, Hamlet Studies, The Upstart Crow, The Virginia Quarterly Review*, etc., and his poems have been published in *Poetry, The New Yorker, The Kenyon Review, The Sewanee Review*, etc.

Richard White is the author of four published novels—and twice as many unpublished ones. His latest book, *A Child in Hamelin*, is probably the first—and last—Catholic novel of the 21st century. He is a member of the English faculty, and writer-in-residence at The Williams School in New London, Connecticut.

Richard Wilbur has published several books of poems, including, recently, *Collected Poems, 1943-2004* (Harvest Books, 2004), and *Mayflies: New*

Poems and Translations (2000). He received the Pulitzer Prize for Poetry in 1957 for his collection *Things of This World* (Harcourt); and, in 1988, he received a second Pulitzer Prize for his *New and Collected Poems* (Harcourt). He has received many awards, including two Bollingen Poetry Prizes, the Wallace Stevens Award, the Aiken Taylor Award for Modern American Poetry, the Frost Medal, the Gold Medal for Poetry from the American Academy of Arts and Letters, the T. S. Eliot Award, the Edna St. Vincent Millay Memorial Award, two PEN translation awards, the Prix de Rome Fellowship. He was elected a chevalier of the *Ordre des Palmes Académiques* and is a former Poet Laureate of the United States. He is Chancellor Emeritus of The Academy of American Poets.

Baron Wormser is the author/co-author of a dozen books including a memoir of his over twenty years living off the grid in rural Maine.

Personal Acknowledgments

Without the help, generosity, and love of many people, I would not have persisted in seeing this book through to publication. I thank the following:

Marilyn Nelson, who had the idea for this book, persuaded me to accept a volunteer task that neither of us imagined would take not months, but years. Marilyn's personal warmth adds to my delight in savoring her awe-inspiring poems.

Nancy and Amy Connellan, who believed in the project, and, during lunches and phone calls, generated potential contributors to add to Marilyn's list.

Gus Mazzocha, graphic artist at the University of Connecticut, who designed a woodcut of Leo for the first publisher. Unfortunately, that wonderfully craggy portrait could not be used. Joe Zanghi, Printed Matter Press, whose layout expertise humanized a challenging process with some helpful answers to my questions. Thanks are also due to Sturgis Haskins for the cover photograph and Arthur Simoes for his portrait photograph of Leo.

All the contributors, many of whom cheered me with their enthusiasm for Leo, and with kind words for my project, in its first and second iterations.

A few contributors deserve special mention. Vivian Shipley, who appreciated, more than I did, the magnitude of my project. Wally Swist, whose voice, on the phone and in his poems, reminds me of my good fortune in connecting with fine poets and their poems. Sandy Phippen, who shared his knowledge about Leo in Maine, and newspaper articles from his files about Leo.

The Connecticut Writing Project Writing Group, teachers all, whose writing talent and critical expertise informs my writing, helps me to persevere, and to smile. Thank you: Shirley Bostrom, Kathy Uschmann, Kay Saur, and Jenny Shaff.

The Portland Library Memoir Writing Group, whose growth as writers is a continual pleasure. Their feedback on my writing is almost as valuable as their good humor and deep friendship. Thanks to each of you: Lonnie Adams, Pat Duffey, Marra Giuliano, Gail Grzegorowicz, Linda Paradis, Deb Susca, and Linda Yohe.

My children, Russell, Siobhan, Brian, and Stephen, who heard, too often, that their mother was working on "the Leo book." Siobhan, especially, knew when to share her expertise as writer, editor, and task divider, and when to provide hugs, pets, or chocolate. Thanks to three daughters-in-law—Susannah, Silvia, and Vicki—for enriching our family. Our grandchildren lighten my life with their presence, their play, and their laughter. Thanks you Clare, Siobhan Julia, and Russell DW; Declan, Johanna, and Cormac; Abigail and Julia. And thank you, God, for the brief, beautiful lives of Cianan DeWeer and Cecilia Lehan. Words are totally inadequate to thank my husband Russ, who, for fifty years, has continued to listen, to love, and to tread softly, always. *Grazie.*

Source Acknowledgments

Axelrod, David B. "In Memoriam, Leo Connellan," in Poetrybay *Online Magazine*, Spring, 2001. with permission of *PoetryBay*, http://www.poetrybay.com

Bradt, David. "An Interview with Leo Connellan," *Connecticut Review*, Spring, 2001, Vol. XXIII, No. 1, with permission of *Connecticut Review*.

Carlson, Gary. "Unique Will Come Later; I'm Leo," *Connecticut Review*, Spring, 2003, with permission of *Connecticut Review*.

Carpenter, William. "Review of *The Maine Poems*," *Maine Times*, November 1, 1999, with permission of the author.

Carruth, Hayden. Excerpt from "Narrative, Anyone?" in *Parnassus Poetry in Review*, Volumes 17, No. 2 and Vol. 18, No. 1, 1990, with permission of the author (6/28/02) and *Parnassus Poetry in Review* (2009).

Connellan, Nancy. "Living with Leo," *Negative Capability*, Vol. XIV, 1 & 2, 1994, with permission of the author and Negative Capability Press.

Corbett, Christopher. "In the Clear Blue Lobster-Water Country With Leo Connellan."An earlier version appeared in *Down East* magazine, November, 1997.

Packard, William. "Leo Connellan: Enormous Heart and Soul," *Negative Capability*, Vol. XIV, 1 & 2, 1994, with permission of the author (6/27/02), and Negative Capability Press.

Packard, William. "Craft Interview #24," *The Poet's Craft: Interviews from The New York Quarterly*. 1987, with permission of the author (6/27/02). Copyright, The New York Quarterly Foundation, Inc.

Phippen, Sanford. "Foreword to *The Maine Poems*, 1999," with permission of the author, and Blackberry Books.

Phippen, Sanford. "Young Poet Continues the Bardic Tradition," *The Ellsworth American*, "Spotlight," February 13-19, 1992, with permission of the author.

Shippee, David. "Connellan in Performance," *Negative Capability*, Vol. XIV, 1 & 2, 1994, with permission of the author, and Negative Capability Press.

Swist, Wally. "*Review of Death in Lobster Land*," *New Haven Advocate*, October, 1978, with permission of the author.

Thibault, Andy. "The Life of the Poet," *Connecticut Magazine*, December, 1995, with permission of the author, and *Connecticut Magazine*.

Wallace, George. "*Crossing America* CD Puts Leo Connellan To Music." *Northport Journal*, May 12 2004, © 2004 Long Islander Newspapers. Reprinted with permission.